ULTIMATE HISTORIC TRAVEL GUIDE

YOUR GUIDE TO HISTORY IN THE OLD WEST

"Eastward I go only by force;
but westward I go free."

—*Henry David Thoreau*

Renowned photographer Edward Curtis's 1904 photograph of seven Navajo riders and a dog crossing Chinle Wash with Canyon de Chelly's sandstone cliffs as a backdrop is one of the most iconic images of the American West.

ULTIMATE
HISTORIC
TRAVEL GUIDE

YOUR GUIDE TO HISTORY
IN THE OLD WEST

From the Publishers of *True West* Magazine

Edited by Stuart Rosebrook

All illustrations by Bob Boze Bell

Maps by Gus Walker, Kevin Kisbey
and Rebecca Edwards

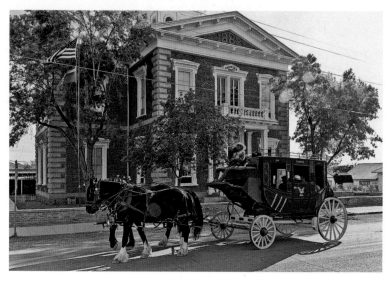

Tombstone hosts numerous annual events in its historic district, including Helldorado Days, held every October since 1929 in honor of the 1879 founding of the infamous mining town.

– COURTESY TOMBSTONE COURTHOUSE STATE HISTORIC PARK –

Executive Editor
Bob Boze Bell

Executive Director
Ken Amorosano

Editor
Stuart Rosebrook

Production Manager
Robert Ray

Graphic Design
Rebecca Edwards
Robert Ray

Copy Editor
Beth Deveny

Map Design
Gus Walker
Kevin Kibsey
Rebecca Edwards

Cover Photography
Chad Coppess
South Dakota
Dept. of Tourism

True West Magazine, P.O. Box 8008, Cave Creek, AZ 85327
TrueWestMagazine.com • 1-888-687-1881

Published by *Two Roads West* | ISBN: 978-0-692-98957-9

The Pacific Coast

The Desert Southwest

Great Basin
and Rocky Mountains

Northern Prairie
and Plains

Southern Prairie
and Plains

DISCOVER WHERE HISTORY HAPPENED AND EXPERIENCE AN OLD WEST ADVENTURE OF A LIFETIME.

"Ocian in view! Oh! The Joy!" William Clark wrote in his journal on November 7, 1805, viewing what he believed was the Pacific Ocean as the Corps of Discovery reached the broad estuary of the Columbia River, 20 miles from the coast.

Clark's exhilaration at reaching the destination the Corps had dreamed of for thousands of treacherous miles is the pure emotion of joy that the editors of *True West* believe our readers— whether first-time visitors or seasoned Western adventurers—discover, and rediscover, when they travel across the American West.

True West's "Ultimate Historic Travel Guide" encourages treks to the West's greatest heritage sites, where you can actually stand and experience where history happened. The editorial staff at *True West* invites you to "saddle up" and travel with us to discover the West together—in the hope we'll inspire your own ultimate Western adventure and make some history of your own.

Custer State Park's Buffalo Roundup of the park's herd has been a public event for over 50 years and is held the last Friday of every September.
– CHAD COPPESS, COURTESY SOUTH DAKOTA TOURISM –

The Pacific Coast

California, Idaho, Nevada, Oregon and Washington

From the Sierra Nevada to the San Juan Islands, from the Columbia River Gorge to Death Valley, the Pacific Coast Region is a land of endless horizons, deep, lush valleys and long snowcapped mountain ranges. The natural beauty, vast distances and diversity of the geology and history of the five states inspire wonderment and admiration for those who lived, explored and settled the region in the centuries before trains, automobiles and airplanes. The heritage of the area is defined by the Pacific Ocean, seemingly endless mountain ranges and the continent's most arid deserts. The Pacific Coast Region is home to dozens of the nation's most recognizable parks, monuments and historic sites, and travelers to the five states find themselves following the trails of explorers, adventurers and pioneers, while walking in the footsteps of missionaries, mountain men and miners.

President Theodore Roosevelt, Glacier Point,
Yosemite National Park, California, 1903

California

Bodie State Historic Park

Visitors who walk the silent streets of Bodie State Historic Park, set amidst the sagebrush of the Sierra Nevada foothills northeast of Yosemite, will discover the real West in the 170 buildings that remain preserved in one of California's most notorious mining camps.

Northeast of Yosemite, 13 miles east of Highway 395 on Bodie Road (Hwy 270), seven miles south of Bridgeport
760-647-6445 • *Parks.CA.gov*

Death Valley National Park

Founded as a monument in 1933, Death Valley National Park's 3.33 million acres in California and Nevada make it the largest park outside of Alaska. Start your tour at the Furnace Creek Visitor Center to visit the nearby Harmony Borax Works and learn about the mineral bonanza that inspired the iconic 20-mule team borax wagons.

Highway 190, Death Valley, CA 92328
760-786-3200 • *NPS.gov*

Donner Memorial State Park

Honoring the tragic emigrant party, Donner Memorial State Park in Donner Pass includes a museum in the visitors center, and a monument dedicated to all the pioneers who traveled to the Golden State on the California Trail.

9 miles west of Truckee, CA
530-582-7892 • *Parks.CA.gov*

El Alisal

Famed author and Western preservationist Charles F. Lummis hand-built his famed cobblestone home in northeast Los Angeles in the late 1890s and early 1900s. Follow up a Lummis house tour with a visit to the Autry Museum of the American West in nearby Griffith Park and, on Saturdays only, Lummis's Historic Southwest Museum in Mt. Washington.

200 E Ave 43, Los Angeles, CA 90031
323-661-9465 • *LAPARKS.org*
Autry.org

Fort Humboldt State Historic Park

Founded in 1853, the outpost was once led by Capt. U.S. Grant, who found it so isolating he left the Army after his posting at Humboldt. Shuttered in 1870, the fort today is open to visitors who can walk the grounds, including the last surviving building—the hospital, now a museum dedicated to Army life and local tribal history.

3431 Fort Ave, Eureka, CA 95503
707-445-6547 • *Parks.CA.gov*

Lava Beds National Monument

Near the Oregon border east of Yreka, California, and south of Klamath Falls, Oregon, Lava Beds National Monument protects the battle sites of the Modoc War, including Captain Jack's Stronghold.

1 Indian Well Campground Trail
Indian Well Hqts, CA 96134
530-667-8100 • *NPS.gov*

Lava Beds National Monument

Fort Humboldt State Park

Marshall Gold State Discovery
State Park

Sutter's Fort State Historic Park

Sacrameto ✪

Donner Pass

Sonoma Barracks

Bodie State Historic Park

★ **San Francisco**

Presidio of San Francisco
National Park

Yosemite National Park, Tioga Pass

Yosemite National Park,
Yosemite Valley

Lone Pine

★ **Fresno**

Death Valley National Park

★ **Bakersfield**

Santa Barbara ★

William S. Hart Ranch & Museum

El Alisal

San Gabriel Mission

★ **Los Angeles**

Old Town
San Diego

San Diego ★

The Spanish founded the Presidio in San Francisco nearly 220 years ago.
The United States Army maintained it as an active fort until 1994. Today,
the Presidio is part of the Golden Gate National Recreation Area.

– COURTESY LIBRARY OF CONGRESS –

Lone Pine

Situated along the Eastern Sierra's "Main Street," U.S. Highway 395, Lone Pine is a historic community first settled in the 1860s. In 1920, Hollywood producers filmed the Western *The Last Roundup* in Lone Pine, and since then over 400 movies and 100 television programs have been produced in and around the distinctive Alabama Hills.

120 South Main St, Lone Pine, CA 93545
760-876-4444
LonePineFilmHistoryMuseum.org

Marshall Gold Discovery State Park

In the heart of "Mother Lode Country," Marshall Gold Discovery State Park near Caloma preserves the site where James W. Marshall found gold in the tailings of Sutter's Mill in January 1848. A living history center, the park includes Marshall's cabin and a replica of the original mill. Rangers and docents provide daily programs at the park. Visitors can even pan for gold.

310 Back St, Coloma, CA 95613
530-622-3470 • *Parks.CA.gov*

Old Sacramento

A national historic landmark district and state historic park, Old Sacramento is a living history center on the banks of the Sacramento River. Visitors can tour the California State Railroad Museum, The Delta King Riverboat, Huntington & Hopkins Hardware, Old Sacramento Schoolhouse Museum, Sacramento History Museum and the Wells Fargo History Museum. Passenger train rides can be enjoyed on the California State Railroad Museum's Sacramento Southern Railroad, which departs from the reconstructed Central Pacific Freight Depot.

2nd St & Capitol Mall
Sacramento, CA 95814 • 916-808-7059
OldSacramento.com

In 1826, Jedediah Smith, with a brigade of mountain men, crossed the Mojave Desert, inlcuding the Mojave National Preserve in California, to the Spanish Mission San Gabriel Arcángel in San Bernardino in 1826, a journey illustrated by Frederic Remington for *Collier's Weekly* in 1906.

– COURTESY LIBRARY OF CONGRESS –

Old Town San Diego State Historic Park

Old Town San Diego State Historic Park celebrates and preserves the Spanish, Mexican and early American heritage of the city. Five original adobe buildings survive in the living history center. Don't miss an opportunity to stay and dine at the historic Cosmopolitan Hotel.

4002 Wallace St, San Diego, CA 92110
619-220-5422 • Parks.CA.gov

Presidio of San Francisco

For nearly 220 years, Spain, Mexico and then the United States garrisoned troops at the Presidio of San Francisco. An active military post until 1994, the Presidio is part of the Golden Gate National Recreation Area. Artillery and military architecture buffs will want to tour one of the nation's finest collections of field armaments and historic buildings.

California Hwy 1
San Francisco, CA 94123
415-561-4700 • NPS.gov

San Gabriel Mission

Padre Junipero Serra's fourth mission, San Gabriel, was founded strategically between San Diego and San Carlos Borromeo in Carmel on September 8, 1771, and has been an active parish for more than 245 years. Visitors should tour the museum and follow the self-guided tours of the historic church and grounds—the same oasis that mountain man Jedediah Smith arrived at in 1826 after crossing the Mojave Desert from the east.

254 S Santa Anita St, San Gabriel, CA 91776 • 626-282-3181
SanGabrielMissionChurch.org

Sonoma Barracks

The California Bear Flag Revolt began in June 1846 at the Sonoma Barracks. The restored barracks, across the

Sutter's Fort, Sacramento, California, 1847
– ILLUSTRATION COURTESY LIBRARY OF CONGRESS –

street from Sonoma's Mission San Francisco Solano, are a part of a park complex that includes General Mariano Guadalupe Vallejo's home, the Toscano Hotel, the Servants' Quarters and the Blue Wing Inn.

Spain Street & First Street East
Sonoma, CA 95476 • 707-935-6832
Parks.CA.gov

Sutter's Fort State Historic Park

In 1839, Swiss pioneer John Sutter received a land grant from Mexico to build a community he called New Helvetia near the confluence of the Sacramento and American rivers. Today, visitors can tour Sutter's Fort State Historic Park, a living history center that includes one of the most significant historic structures in the state, the fully restored Sutter's Fort.

2701 L St, Sacramento, CA 95816
916-445-4422 • Parks.CA.gov

William S. Hart Ranch and Museum

Silent movie star William S. Hart's Spanish Colonial Revival-style mansion, built on his ranch in 1910 in Newhall, north of Los Angeles, is dedicated to Hart's life in the movies. Hart is famous for saying: "When I was making pictures, the people gave me their nickels, dimes and quarters. When I am gone, I want them to have my home."

24151 Newhall Ave, Newhall, CA 91321
661-254-4584 • HartMuseum.org

Black Bart's Bad Day

November 3, 1883

It's a Saturday as the Sonora-Milton stage rattles along, empty, save for the driver. Reason E. McConnell has been on the road for three hours since he stopped at the Patterson Mine, near Tuttletown, California, picking up $4,200 worth of amalgamated gold. The Wells Fargo box also contains $500 in gold coin and $64 in raw gold.

McConnell finally reins up in front of the Reynolds Ferry Hotel, nestled along the banks of the Stanislaus River. Jimmy Rolleri, the hotel manager's 19-year-old son, exits the hotel and exchanges the outgoing mail for the incoming. Glancing at the empty coach, Rolleri asks if he can catch a ride up the hill on the opposite side of the river. A traveler who had stopped at the hotel the previous night reported seeing "two big bucks up there on the flat above Yaqui Gulch," he says.

McConnell tells the boy to grab his gun, and Rolleri returns with a "well-worn but serviceable .44 Henry rifle." With the help of Henry Requa, the two successfully ferry the stage across the river. Requa returns the ferry to the hotel side of the river, and Rolleri jumps up on the box with McConnell, who slaps the reins of his team, encouraging them up the steep approach to Funk Hill.

Halfway up the long grade, Rolleri asks McConnell to slow down. He jumps off

with his rifle, thanks McConnell for the lift and heads out into the underbrush to hunt for the big bucks.

The six-horse team continues on, struggling up the steep grade for another 30 minutes. As the stage rounds the head of Yaqui Gulch, with the ridge line in sight, the lead horses snort and rear in fright when a lone, hooded figure, shotgun in hand, leaps into the roadway.

Wearing a dirt-smudged duster and a flour sack with eye holes cut into them, the highwayman demands the Wells Fargo box be thrown down. McConnell informs the robber it's bolted down. The outlaw tells the driver to unhitch his team, but McConnell protests, fearing the stage will roll down the hill due to its bad brakes. The robber's solution is for McConnell to wedge rocks behind the wheels, but the driver brashly pushes his luck by stating, "Why don't you do it?"

Incredibly, the hooded robber keeps his shotgun trained on the driver, picks up several stones and blocks the back wheels. McConnell then unhitches the team and leads it uphill. "If you don't want to get shot," the robber warns him, "don't come back or even look back in this direction for at least one hour." While leading the team, McConnell hears the robber banging away at the strongbox. Sneaking glances toward the coach, he can't see the brigand, who has probably crawled into the stagecoach.

Reason McConnell was driving a "mud wagon," like this one, on Funk Hill. It had wider wheels for better traction in the mountains and foothills of California and Oregon.

– TRUE WEST ARCHIVES –

Two hundred yards from the stage, McConnell stops to catch his breath when downhill movement catches his eye. It's Jimmy Rolleri, the Henry rifle in the crook of his arm, moving across an open swale of land about 300 yards below. Tying his team to an oak tree, McConnell runs downhill as quietly as he can, frantically waving his hat until he gets Rolleri's attention. Coming up the hill, Rolleri first thinks McConnell has discovered the deer. But the driver fills him in on the situation, and the two warily approach the stage with the intent of capturing the outlaw, or killing him. When they get within 100 yards, the bandit suddenly emerges from the stage and spots them. The outlaw throws a sack over his shoulder and starts to run.

McConnell borrows Rolleri's rifle and fires twice, missing the robber both times.

"Here, let me shoot," young Rolleri says. "I'll get him and I won't kill him, either." With Rolleri's shot, the outlaw stumbles, but he vanishes into the underbrush with his booty.

When the county sheriff and a Wells Fargo detective arrive, they discover what the brigand left behind in his hasty retreat: a derby hat, three pairs of cuffs, an opera glass case and a silk crepe handkerchief with the laundry mark "F.X.O.7." on it.

After eight years and 28 successful stage holdups, this last item will prove to be Black Bart's undoing. ★

Recommended:
Black Bart: Boulevardier Bandit by George Hoeper, published by Word Dancer Press; *and Lawman: The Life and Times of Harry Morse, 1835-1912* by John Boessenecker, published by University of Oklahoma Press.

– COURTESY RICHARD ROLLERI –

– COURTESY WELLS FARGO BANK –

Poetic Justice: Young Jimmy Rolleri (top left) fires the shot that wings Black Bart (top right) and forces him to leave behind the handkerchief with a laundry stamp—a clue that Wells Fargo Detective Harry Morse (above) parlays into a collar.

– ILLUSTRATION BY BOB BOZE BELL –

In 1868, Timothy H. O'Sullivan accompanied the Clarence King Survey of the 40th Parallel across the Great Basin. O'Sullivan's images of the Snake River, Shoshone Canyon and Falls remain some of his finest images, many of which captured the geology and fellow members of the survey party, providing scale to the immensity of the scene.

– COURTESY LIBRARY OF CONGRESS –

Yosemite National Park

On June 30, 1864, President Abraham Lincoln signed the Yosemite Grant, protecting Yosemite Valley and the Mariposa Grove. A national park since 1890, Yosemite was a favorite of naturalist John Muir and President Theodore Roosevelt, and was originally patrolled by the U.S. Cavalry.

PO Box 577, Yosemite National Park, CA 95389 • 209-372-0200 • *NPS.gov*

Idaho

Fort Hall Replica

New England entrepreneur Nathaniel Wyeth built Fort Hall in 1832 to support his fur trade business. The fort evolved to become a key crossroads and supply center on the Oregon Trail. Today, Fort Hall Replica, "the gateway to the Pacific," is a living history center dedicated to Indian, fur trade and Oregon Trail history.

3000 Avenue of the Chiefs Pocatello, ID 83204 • 208-234-1795 *FortHall.net*

Idaho City

In Boise Basin, Idaho City was the "Queen of the Gold Camps," the center of the richest gold strikes in the history of the American Northwest in the 1860s. Today, visitors to the village can walk the boardwalks of the boomtown and visit numerous historic buildings, including the

Boise Basin Historical Museum housed in the original post office built in 1867.

208-392-4159 • *IdahoCity.org*

Nez Perce National Historical Park

A multi-state national park, Nez Perce National Historical Park has six sites in Idaho, as well. The Spalding Site, near Lapwai, is the headquarters of the park, and has a visitors center and museum.

39063 U.S. 95, Lapwai, ID 83540 208-843-7009 • *NPS.gov*

Old Fort Boise

Originally a Hudson Bay outpost at the confluence of the Boise and Snake rivers, a small monument marks the site of the Old Fort Boise in the Fort Boise Wildlife Management Area. A replica of the old fort was built as a living history center in Parma, and includes a museum and a pioneer cabin.

Parma, ID 83660 • 208-722-5210 *OldFortBoise.com*

Coeur d'Alene's Old Mission State Park

Built by Catholic Jesuit missionaries and local Coeur d'Alene Indians between 1850 and 1853, the Mission of the Sacred Heart at Coeur d'Alene's Old Mission State Park is the oldest building in Idaho. Tour the mission, a restored parish house and the historic cemetery. Exhibits interpret the history

FIRST PHOTO OF YOSEMITE

Charles Leander Weed was an early Sacramento, California, photographer.
Entrepreneur James Hutching brought Weed to Yosemite to be the first
photographer to take images of the spectacular valley in June 1859, including
Yosemite Falls from the south bank of the Merced River.

– COURTESY UC BERKELEY, BANCROFT LIBRARY –

Coeur d'Alene — Old Mission State Park
Wallace
Moscow
Nez Perce National Historic Park
Salmon
Yankee Fork State Park
Idaho City
Boise
Old Fort Boise — Rock Creek Station
Idaho Falls
Fort Hall Replica

northern panhandle. Start your walking tour of the Wallace Historic District at the Wallace District Mining Museum, and continue on to the Oasis Bordello Museum and the Northern Pacific Depot Museum. Don't leave town without taking the Sierra Silver Mine Tour.

208-753-7151 • *Wallace-ID.com*

Land of Yankee Fork State Park

One of Idaho's premier historic state parks, Land of Yankee Fork State Park in Round Valley has several historic sites, including three ghost towns—Bayhorse, Bonanza and Custer—and the Yankee Fork Gold Dredge; plus the Shoshone Indian mid-1800s Challis Bison Kill site. Visitors should start in Challis at the interpretive center before touring the park.

Junction of U.S. 93 and State Highway 75
Challis, ID • 208-879-5244
ParksAndRecreation.Idaho.gov

Nevada

California Trail Interpretive Center

Ever wondered what it was like to cross the nation in a Conestoga wagon? Or to walk across the continent to find your bonanza of gold in California? The California Trail Interpretive Center near Elko will answer all your questions with outstanding exhibitions and regular living history events.

1 Interpretive Center Way
Elko, NV 89801 • 775-738-1849
CaliforniaTrailCenter.org

Carson City Historic District

Named after famed Westerner Kit Carson by the city's founder Abraham V.Z. Curry in 1858, Carson City quickly became a crossroads of emigrants, prospectors, soldiers and entrepreneurs following the California Trail. Chosen as the Territorial capital city in 1861, Carson City has an extensive historic

of Catholic missionary efforts in the Rocky Mountains.

3715 E 3200 N, Hansen, ID 83334
208-432-4000
ParksAndRecreation.Idaho.gov

Rock Creek Station

An Idaho Historical Society living history center, Rock Creek Station and the Stricker Home were built in 1865. An important transportation hub along the Oregon Trail south of Hansen, the historic trail stop also includes a pioneer cemetery and interpretive center.

3715 E 3200 N, Hansen, ID 83334
208-432-4000 • *History.Idaho.gov*

Salmon

Salmon is a jewel in the valley near the confluence of the Salmon and Lehmi rivers along the Lewis and Clark National Historic Trail on U.S. 93. A traditional home of the Shoshone tribe, the City of Salmon is home to the Sacajawea Interpretive, Cultural and Educational Center, which is dedicated to the heritage and history of the region.

208-756-2100 • *VisitSalmonValley.com*

Wallace

Located in the richest silver district in American history, Wallace is in the Silver Valley of Shoshone County in Idaho's

Photographer Timothy H. O'Sullivan dramatically captured Lt. George M. Wheeler's survey route up the Colorado River, including this camp on Mirror Bar, Black Canyon, Nevada Territory, in 1871.

district, including the Capitol grounds, Nevada State Railroad Museum and Nevada State Museum in the former U.S. Mint, and a neighborhood of the Silver State's 19th-century homes, which visitors can enjoy by taking the self-guided Blue Line Trail. Day trips from Carson City should include visits to Nevada's oldest settlement, Genoa, and the historic town of Dayton.

775-577-2345 • *VisitCarsonCity.com*

Fort Churchill State Historic Park

When settlement expanded in Nevada in the late 1850s, the Army built a series of forts across the Central Overland Route in the territory to protect settlers, mail carriers, freight trains and emigrants traveling the new central route across the Great Basin. Fort Churchill State Historic Park has an excellent walking tour of the ruins of the fort, where troops were posted from 1860 to 1869.

Silver Springs, NV 89429
775-577-2345 • *Parks.NV.gov*

Old Las Vegas Mormon Fort State Historic Park

In the shadow of the neon lights and towering casinos of the Las Vegas Strip stands Old Las Vegas Mormon Fort State Historic Park, an Old West living

Wyatt Earp arrived in the new boomtown of Tonapah in January of 1902. He was fresh from his Alaska adventure and no doubt had some capital to invest. He went with what he knew, saloons, and financed one.

KIT CARSON

Few men in the 19th-century traveled as extensively in the West as Kit Carson. Between 1843 and 1845, Carson guided John C. Frémont three times on cross-country surveys, including two treks across the future state of Nevada to California. Nevada's state capital, Carson City, is named in honor of the intrepid explorer.

history center dedicated to the Mormon missionaries' community built in 1855. While the first American settlement at Vegas Springs only lasted until 1857, the settlement left behind became the humble beginnings of the internationally famous desert city.

500 E Washington Ave, Las Vegas, NV 89101 • 702-486-3511 • Parks.NV.gov

Tonapah Historic Mining Park

Interested in Old West mining history? Take a slow drive from Las Vegas to the Tonapah Historic Mining Park on U.S. 95 and plan on stops at the ghost towns of Rhyolite near Beatty, Gold Point near Lida, and Goldfield and Belmont outside of Tonapah. In addition to the mining park, Tonapah has a walking tour of its historic buildings.

110 Burro Ave, Tonopah, NV 89049
775-482-9274
TonapahHistoricMiningPark.com

Virginia City

In the desert hills between Reno and Carson City, one of the richest silver strikes in U.S. history, the Comstock Lode, rocketed Nevada from territory to statehood. Today, Virginia City is a virtual Victorian-era heritage center, with historic sites, museums and buildings. Don't miss the Storey County Courthouse, Piper Opera House, Virginia & Truckee Railroad, the Comstock Mill, Ponderosa Mine Tour, Mark Twain Museum and the Comstock Fire Museum. A great way to see the historic mining camp is aboard the Virginia City Trolley tour.

775-847-1114 • VirginiaCityNV.com

Ward Charcoal Ovens State Historic Park

After visiting the historic mining community of Ely, Nevada, located on U.S. 50 ("the loneliest road in America"), including an excursion on the historic passenger trains of the Nevada Northern Railway Museum, travel southeast to a unique site from Nevada's storied mining history—the Ward Charcoal Ovens. The thirty-foot-high kilns were built to support the smelting operations of lead in the long-gone mining town of Ward.

Ely, NV 89315 • 775-289-1693
Parks.NV.gov

Oregon
The Dalles

A tribal fishing center and crossroads of the Columbia River history for centuries, The Dalles developed as an American community at the terminus of the Oregon Trail and launching point for emigrant rafting parties down the river to the Willamette River Valley. While an alternate overland route was built over the Blue Mountains and around Mt. Hood to Oregon City, The Dalles remained an important economic and transportation hub. Today, visitors should begin their visit at Fort Dalles and then tour the world-class Columbia River Gorge Discovery Center.

404 W 2nd St, The Dalles, OR 97058
541-296-2231 • *TheDallesChamber.com*
HistoricTheDalles.org

Fort Clatsop National Memorial

Lewis and Clark National Historical Park has sites on both sides of the Columbia River, in Oregon and Washington, as it nears the Pacific Ocean, including Fort Clatsop National Memorial, the winter encampment of the Corps of Discovery. The centerpiece of Fort Clatsop, just south of the historic port city Astoria, is the replica of the fort that is supported by a very active ranger program with period-costumed presentations throughout the summer and a visitors center.

92343 Fort Clatsop Rd
Astoria, OR 97103
503-861-2471 • *NPS.gov*

Fort Stevens State Park

At the mouth of the Columbia River, a visitor to Fort Stevens State Park can watch the modern ships ply the Columbia River Bar, a treacherous navigation that has claimed over 2,000 ships, earning it the moniker "graveyard of the Pacific." Because it was an active fort from the Civil War through World War II, a tour of the park's historic sites reveals Fort Stevens' nearly 90 years of history. After a tour of the park, visit Astoria's Columbia River Maritime Museum to learn about the dramatic history of sailing and shipping on the Columbia River.

100 Peter Iredale Rd
Hammond, OR 97121 • 503-861-3170
OregonStateParks.org / CRMM.org

Historic Oregon City

Oregon City welcomes visitors to its historic park, educational history center and museum, like it welcomed the trail-weary Oregon Trail travelers who survived the transcontinental trip and the final leg—the descent over the Cascade Range past Mt. Hood into the Willamette Valley. Tour the Visitor Center, End of the Oregon Trail Interpretive Center, the Country Store and the Heritage Garden. While in Oregon City, plan on extra time to visit the historic Barclay, McLoughlin and Holmes Houses, and tour downtown.

1726 Washington St
Oregon City, OR 97405 • 503-657-9336
HistoricOregonCity.org / NPS.gov

Oregon Trail National Trail Center

Near Baker City, the Bureau of Land Management's Oregon Trail National Trail Center is dedicated to interpreting history through exhibits and ranger-led programs, many in period costume, explaining the history and experiences of the thousands of emigrants who made the overland journey across the country on the Oregon Trail.

22267 OR-86, Baker City, OR 97814
541-523-1843
OregonTrail.BLM.gov

The year 1922 brought acclaim to Mabel Strickland: she not only won as all-around cowgirl at Cheyenne Frontier Days, she also tied for first as the trick riding champion at the Madison Square Garden rodeo. In 1927, she set a steer roping record at the Pendleton Round-Up (she's shown above roping a steer in the Oregon arena).

– TRUE WEST ARCHIVES –

Pendleton

Pendleton is world famous for the Pendleton Round-Up, a rodeo equally known for its action in the arena as well as its dedication to the local Indian cultures and American settlement history of the Umatilla River Valley. Visitors will enjoy touring the Pendleton Woolen Mills, Round-Up and Happy Canyon Hall of Fame Museum, Heritage Station Museum and Tamástslikt Cultural Institute. Before leaving town, don't miss Hamley's & Co., a famous saddle and Western wear shop downtown, in business since 1883.

501 S Main, Pendleton, OR 97801
541-276-7411 • TravelPendleton.com

Pioneer Courthouse

The oldest federal building in the Pacific Northwest and second-oldest west of the Mississippi, the Pioneer Courthouse in Pioneer Square in Portland opened in 1869. Just down the street is the Oregon Historical Society Museum, with comprehensive exhibits on the heritage, history and diverse cultures that have defined Oregon history.

700 SW 6th Ave, Portland, OR 97204
503-833-5300
PioneerCourthouse.org / OHS.org

Washington
Cape Disappointment State Park

On Washington's Long Beach Peninsula at the mouth of the Columbia River across from Fort Stevens State Park in Oregon, Cape Disappointment State Park is a beautiful place to walk in the footsteps of Lewis and Clark's Corps of Discovery. Take a tour of the Lewis and Clark Interpretive Center and learn about their expedition and local Native culture. Also, don't miss a hike out to the North Head Lighthouse, built in 1897-'98, that is still aiding ships navigating the Columbia River Bar.

244 Robert Gray Dr, Ilwaco, WA 98624
360-642-3078 • Parks.WA.gov

Fort Columbia
Historical State Park

East of Cape Disappointment and part of the national and state park consortium of the Lewis and Clark National Historical Park, Columbia State Historical Park at the Chinook Point Historical Landmark was a U.S. Army Coastal Artillery fort from 1896 to 1947. Visitors will enjoy touring the historic officer's house, the observation station and an interpretive center.

U.S. Highway 101, Chinook, WA 98614
360-816-6230 • Parks.WA.gov

Fort Vancouver
National Historic Site

Fort Vancouver National Historic Site in Vancouver, Washington, is a significant British and American outpost in the Northwest. The English Hudson Bay Company built the fort in 1824 and until the 1840s it was the largest European community on the West Coast. The U.S. Army occupied the fort in 1849 and until 2011 maintained an Army Reserve and Washington National Guard unit at the base. Visitors will enjoy the museum and living history programs, which tell the fascinating story of the fur trade and settlement of the Northwest.

612 E Reserve St
Vancouver, WA 98661
360-816-6230 • NPS.gov

Klondike Gold Rush
National Historical Park

The Seattle unit of the Klondike Gold Rush National Historical Park complements the park's sites in Skagway, Alaska, in interpreting the 1898 gold rush that was the greatest mineral bonanza on the West Coast since the California Gold Rush of 1849. The park's visitors center, located

within the Pioneer Square National Historic District in downtown Seattle, offers walking tours and living history programs, as well as a series of permanent and temporary exhibitions interpreting the history of the stampede to the Klondike.

319 2nd Ave S, Seattle, WA 98104
206-220-4240 • NPS.gov

San Juan Island
National Historical Park

Located in Puget Sound, San Juan Island National Historical Park interprets the conflict that almost drew Great Britain and the United States into war over the death of a pig in 1859. The American Camp Visitor Center and the English Camp Visitor Center provide historical interpretation of the history of the island and the international dispute over the San Juan Islands.

4668 Cattle Point Rd, Friday Harbor, WA 98250 • 360-378-2240 • NPS.gov

Steptoe Battlefield State Park

The Steptoe Battlefield State Park commemorates a May 1858 battle between Col. Edward Steptoe's U.S. troops and a combined force of Spokane, Palouse, Coeur d'Alene and Yakama tribes. The 160 soldiers, on a march from Fort Walla Walla to Fort Colville, were surprised by the Indians and forced to retreat through a series of skirmishes, barely escaping. The

Fort Vancouver, Washington Territory, 1855

four-acre park near Rosalia has a monument to the battle and interpretive signs telling the story of the conflict.

South Summit Loop, Rosalia, WA 99170
509-337-6457 • Parks.WA.gov

Whitman Mission National Historic Site

The Whitman Mission National Historic Site preserves and interprets the location of a significant settlement and event in U.S. Western history. Among the first emigrants from the Eastern United States were Methodist missionaries Dr. Marcus and Mrs. Narcissa Prentiss Whitman, who arrived in 1836. The Whitmans' mission was the site of the Whitman Massacre in 1847, a controversial event that dramatically changed the course of history in the American Northwest between settlers and local tribes. After touring the mission grounds, take a short drive to Walla Walla and tour Fort

Visitors to Oregon and Washington will discover how the Columbia River Gorge defined the region's cultural and settlement history.

Walla Walla Museum for interactive exhibits and living history programs on the fort and region's history.

328 Whitman Mission Rd
Walla Walla, WA 99362
509-522-6360 • NPS.gov / FWWM.org

Great Books

American Trinity: Jeffferson, Custer, and the Spirit of the West *by Larry Len Peterson* (Far Country Press, 2017)

California: A History *by Kevin Starr* (The Modern Library, 2007)

Chief Joseph: Guardian of the People *by Candy Moulton* (Forge, 2006)

Junipero Serra: California's Founding Father *by Stephen Hackel* (Hill and Wang, 2013)

Roughing It *by Mark Twain* (Signet Classics, 2008)

Siskiyou Trail: The Hudson's Bay Company route to California *by Richard H. Dillon* (McGraw Hill, 1975)

So Rugged and Mountainous: Blazing the Trails to Oregon and California, 1812–1848 *by Will Bagley* (University of Oklahoma Press, 2010)

Spirit in the Rock: The Fierce Battle for Modoc Homelands *by Jim Compton* (Washington State University Press, 2017)

The American Fur Trade of the Fart West, Volume 1 *by Hiram Martin Chittenden* (Bison Books, 1986)

The Journals of Lewis and Clark *edited by Bernard DeVoto, foreword by Stephen Ambrose* (Houghton Mifflin, 1997)

The Saga of Ben Holliday: Giant of the Old West *by Ella Lucia* (Hastings House, 1959)

The Modoc War: A Story of Genocide at the Dawn of America's Gilded Age *by Robert Aquinas McNally* (Bison Books, 2017)

The Spanish Frontier in North America *by David J. Weber* (Yale University Press, 1992)

Thunder in the Mountains: Chief Joseph, Oliver Otis Howard, and the Nez Perce War *by Daniel Sharfstein* (W.W. Norton, 2016)

Undaunted Courage: Meriwether Lewis, Thomas Jefferson, and the Opening of the American West *by Stephen Ambrose* (Simon & Schuster, 1997)

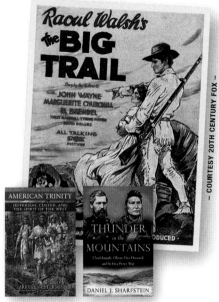

— COURTESY 20TH CENTURY FOX —

Western Film & TV

Bend of the River (*Universal, 1952*)

Bonanza (*NBC, 1959-1973*)

Death Valley Days (*Flying A Productions, 1952-1970*)

I Will Fight No More Forever (*ABC, 1975*)

McCabe and Mrs. Miller (*Warner Bros., 1971*)

Meek's Cutoff (*Evenstar Films, 2010*)

Ride the High Country (*MGM, 1962*)

River of No Return (*20th Century Fox, 1954*)

Seven Alone (*ABC, 1974*)

The Ballad of Cable Hogue (*Warner Bros., 1970*)

The Big Trail (*Fox, 1931*)

The Far Horizons (*Paramount, 1955*)

The Oregon Trail (*20th Century Fox, 1955*)

The Way West (*United Artists, 1967*)

Zorro (*ABC, 1957-1959*)

In the 1870s and 1880s, more than 40 men lost their lives fighting on the only street of this peaceful-looking adobe village, Lincoln, New Mexico Territory. The building at center, above, is the Murphy-Dolan store, known locally as "The House," which later did duty as the Lincoln County Courthouse. James Dolan and Henry McCarty (who will also become known as Henry Antrim, William H. Bonney, Billy Bonney, Kid, the Kid, Kid Antrim, Billy Kid and Billy the Kid) will figure prominently in the history of the building and the town.

– COURTESY ROBERT G. MCCUBBIN COLLECTION –

Moran's Point, Grand Canyon,
Arizona Territory, circa 1903
– COURTESY LIBRARY OF CONGRESS –

The Desert Southwest

Arizona, New Mexico, Oklahoma and Texas

From the Grand Canyon to the Texas Gulf Coast, from the Rio Grande River Valley to Oklahoma's endless grasslands, the Desert Southwest Region is a land of sky islands, spectacular canyon lands, plains and prairies, unforgiving deserts and rugged mountains. The natural beauty, vast distances, and diversity of cultures in the regions will inspire the visitor to gain a greater understanding of how the aridity of the Sonoran and Chihuahuan deserts has influenced the Indian, Hispanic and American settlement of the region. The Desert Southwest Region is home to many of the nation's most recognizable geologic landmarks, ancient pueblos, monuments and historic sites, but also some of its oldest Indian and Hispanic communities. Visitors to the four states will quickly find themselves on the trails of conquistadores and explorers, cowboys and cavalry, and walking in the footsteps of ancient peoples, Indian nations, homesteaders and prospectors.

Arizona

Battle of Big Dry Wash Site

In July 1882, the last bloody battle between Army regulars and the Apache tribe took place north of Payson and is commemorated by a marker built in the 1930s by the U.S. Forest Service and the Civilian Conservation Corps. To visit the battle site from Payson, drive north on Highway 87 through Pine and Strawberry to the Rim Road, Forest Road 300. Turn right and drive east to the Battle of Big Dry Wash Historical Marker near General Springs.

Battle of Big Dry Wash Site, Payson, AZ
928-472-5110 • *RimCountryMuseums.com*

Camp Verde State Historic Park

Founded in 1865, Camp Verde State Historic Park is a living history center that commemorates and honors the history of the Army and the conflict with the Yavapai and Western Apaches during the American settlement of Central Arizona.

125 E Hollamon St
Camp Verde, AZ 86322
928-567-3275
AZStateParks.com

Canyon de Chelly National Monument

Located in the heart of the Navajo Reservation, Canyon de Chelly National Monument is home to the traditional clans who have lived in the specatacular canyon for generations. Tour the national monument, above and below the canyon, with special guided tours of the park, and learn about the canyon's importance to Navajo culture, and the tragic years of the tribe's incarceration at Bosque Redondo in New Mexico.

PO Box 588, Chinle, AZ 86503
928-674-5500 • *NPS.gov*

Fort Apache Historic Park

A key outpost during the U.S. Army's conflict with the Apaches from the 1860s to the 1880s, Fort Apache today is part of the Theodore Roosevelt National Historic Landmark, maintained by the Apache Tribe with assistance from the Fort Apache Heritage Foundation. The park offers exhibits on tribal history plus a museum shop. The Nohwike' Bágowa (House of Our Footprints) Museum is open six days a week, and on Sundays May through September.

127 Scout St, Fort Apache, AZ 85926
928-338-1392 • *FortApacheArizona.org*

Fort Bowie National Historic Site

Located at Apache Springs near the national stageroad in the heart of Chiricahua territory, Fort Bowie National

Grand Canyon National Park

Canyon de Chelly National Monument

★ Flagstaff • Holbrook

Prescott • • Fort Whipple

Camp Verde State Historic Park •

• Battle of Big Dry Wash Site

Quartermaster's Depot State Historic Park

✪ Phoenix

• Fort Apache Historic Park

★ Yuma

Yuma Territorial Prison State Historic Park

• Picacho Peak State Historic Park

★ Tucson

Warren Earp's Grave • • Fort Bowie National Historic Site

Bisbee ★ • Tombstone

Queen Mine

Tubac Presidio State Historic Park

Slaughter Ranch

Fort Bowie was one of the first of many military camps that sprang into being as a result of hostilities between whites and the earlier inhabitants of the Southwest, including those who now are referred to as Apaches. While a great boost to the local economy, these garrisons, along with field operations, cost the federal government vast sums of tax dollars and achieved only limited results to bring order to the tumultuous Southwest.

– COURTESY NATIONAL ARCHIVES –

Historic Site can be reached by a short hike across the Butterfield Trail, past the spring and through the desert hills to well-maintained ruins of the fort and historic cemetery.

3500 S Apache Pass Rd
Bowie, AZ 85605
520-847-2500 • NPS.gov

Fort Whipple

Founded in 1863, Fort Whipple was one of the Army's earliest outposts in central and Northern Arizona during the American post-Civil War settlement of the Grand Canyon state. Gen. George Crook built the Crook Trail from Whipple to Fort Apache during the Yavapai War. Today, a historic museum is maintained in a 1909 officer's home on the post's grounds, which today is a V.A. Hospital for Northern Arizona.

AZ-89, Prescott, AZ 86303
928-445-3122 • Sharlot.org

Grand Canyon National Park

The Grand Canyon is the traditional home and a sacred site to the Havasupai, Hualapai, Navajo, Hopi and Paiute Indians of northern Arizona. Grand Canyon National Park's South Rim visitors center receives 5 million visitors annually. Don't miss the exhibition on John Wesley Powell's exploration of the Grand Canyon and his epic 1869 river run on the Green-Colorado.

PO Box 129 Grand Canyon, AZ 86023
928-638-7888 • NPS.gov

Holbrook

Founded in 1881 by the Santa Fe Railway, Holbrook quickly gained a reputation as one of the toughest towns in the Southwest. As the headquarters of the infamous Aztec Land & Cattle Company, aka the Hashknife Outfit, a walking/driving tour of the historic town once patrolled by legendary lawman Sheriff Commodore

Texas John Slaughter was the first outlaw New Mexico Territorial Gov. Lew Wallace wanted to round up. (Billy the Kid was 14th on his list.) Slaughter's first killing, of drunken rustler Barney Gallagher, took place while he was herding cattle on John Chisum's ranch in New Mexico in September 1876. By 1880, Slaughter was ranching in Arizona near the border with Mexico. In 1886, he became Cochise County sheriff. This circa 1890s photograph captures Slaughter as the quintessential cowboy lawman.

– TRUE WEST ARCHIVES –

Perry Owens starts at the Historic Navajo County Courthouse.

928-524-6558 • *Cl.Holbrook.US.az*

Picacho Peak State Historic Park

Just off Interstate 10, south of Casa Grande, the picturesque Picacho Peak can be seen for miles in every direction, a landmark for generations of travelers and the site of the Westernmost battle of the Civil War on April 15, 1862. Every March re-enactors gather and entertain thousands with a re-enactment of three battles: Picacho Peak, Glorieta and Val Verde, the latter two fought in New Mexico.

I-10, Exit 219, Eloy, AZ 85141
520-466-3183 • *AZStateParks.com*

Prescott

The historic and picturesque Territorial capital of Arizona, Prescott is the perfect town in which to take a walk through state history. Start at Sharlot Hall Museum, the living history center with several historic buildings, including the Territorial Governor's Home, and walk down Gurley Street to Prescott's historic Courthouse Square, where Solon Borglum's *Rough Rider* bronze greets visitors to the park. Across the street take a walk down Montezuma Avenue, known as Whiskey Row, and visit the historic Palace Saloon.

928-445-2000 • *Prescott.org*

Queen Mine

The centerpiece historical site in downtown Bisbee is Phelps Dodge's

Queen Mine, one of the richest mineral bonanzas in state history. Retired miners lead the underground tours that take visitors on trams deep into the copper mine. After touring the mine, don't miss an opportunity to walk through Bisbee's historic district, including a tour of the Bisbee Mining and Historical Museum, and the legendary Copper Queen Hotel.

478 N Dart Rd, Bisbee, AZ 85603
520-432-2071 • *QueenMineTour.com*
DiscoverBisbee.com

Slaughter Ranch

Texas John Slaughter was a legendary lawman and rancher in southeastern Arizona during and after the Apache Wars and Earp-Cowboy feuds in Cochise County in the late 19th century. Today his San Bernardino Ranch is home to the Johnson Historical Museum of Southern Arizona and adjacent to the San Bernardino National Wildlife Refuge.

6153 Geronimo Trail, Douglas, AZ 85607
520-678-7596 • *SlaughterRanch.com*

Tombstone

"The town to tough to die," Tombstone is Arizona's most infamous Territorial mining camp and is known internationally for the Earp Clanton gunfight behind the O.K. Corral. Tour the Tombstone County Courthouse State Historic Park, take a walk through Boothill Graveyard, and park at one end of Allen Street and walk into history. In the National Historic District don't miss visiting Big Nose Kate's Saloon, the Crystal Palace, C.S. Fly's, O.K. Corral, the Bird Cage Saloon, Rose Tree Museum, Good Enough Mine Underground Tour and the *Tombstone Epitaph Museum.*

888-457-3929 • *TombstoneChamber.com*

Tubac Presidio State Historic Park

Tubac Presidio was the first Spanish fort in present-day Arizona. In 1752,

MORGAN EARP

WARREN EARP

VIRGIL EARP

WYATT EARP

Forty-five-year-old Warren Earp, the youngest of the Earp brothers, was gunless when cowboy Johnny Boyette shot him through the heart outside Brown's Saloon in Willcox, Arizona, on July 9, 1900.

– TRUE WEST ARCHIVES –

Behind the O.K. Corral

October 26, 1881

Come along," Virgil Earp says, handing a Wells, Fargo shotgun to Doc Holliday. The quartet starts up Fourth Street, walking four abreast, but when they turn the corner at Fremont Street, they walk two by two, favoring the south sidewalk.

Striding purposefully past the rear entrance to the O.K. Corral, the quartet sees Cochise County Sheriff John Behan coming toward them. "Hold up boys, don't go down there or there will be trouble!"

Virgil is firm about enforcing the ordinance banning guns within the city limits. "Johnny, I am going down to disarm them," he tells the sheriff.

"I have been down there to disarm them!" Behan cries. Both Wyatt and Virgil resheath their weapons. In spite of Behan's claim, they continue on, perhaps to meet their tormentors face to face and tell them off.

But as they step into the lot, it is apparent that Behan was not quite telling the truth. Both Billy Clanton and Frank McLaury have on holsters with their pistols in plain sight.

"Boys, throw up your hands," Virgil demands. "I want your guns."

Nervous about the confrontation and sensing the bristling attitude of Morgan Earp and Doc Holliday, Frank McLaury says, "We will," and makes a motion to pull his revolver. Holliday makes a sudden move toward Tom McLaury, thrusting the shotgun at him in a threatening manner. Wyatt Earp jerks his pistol from his coat pocket, and Billy Clanton pulls his revolver.

"Hold on, I don't want that!" says Virgil, realizing the situation is slipping from his control.

Two shots ring out, almost as one. Then a long pause. Frank McLaury clutches his stomach and staggers, as the firing becomes general (Ike Clanton flees once the shooting starts).

Some 30 shots are fired in less than 30 seconds. The most famous and over-analyzed fight in the West is over. The repercussions are only beginning.

★

The Fremont Street confrontation has been brewing for some time as the Earps and Holliday finally give Ike Clanton his wish: "All I want is four feet of ground."

The fight ends in the middle of Fremont Street as Morgan Earp (rising to one knee) and Doc Holliday face Frank McLaury, who says to Doc, "I've got you now." Doc replies, "Blaze away! You're a daisy if you do." Both Morgan and Doc fire, sending Frank crashing into the dirt.

In the summer of 1885, Gen. George Crook briefly stayed at Fort Bayard to track Apache raiders taking refuge in New Mexico's Black Range, before crossing into Mexico. The staff officers and their families shown at the fort in 1887 found garrison life a lot easier after Geronimo's surrender the previous year.

following a revolt by local native peoples, Spain placed a fortress, the San Ignacio de Tubac, in the Santa Cruz River Valley. Tubac is famous for being the launch point of the Anza Expedition to San Francisco in 1775. By 1787, the fort was manned by the same native peoples who had revolted, now enlisted as a Spanish infantry company at Tubac. The Tubac Presidio would later become headquarters for Charles Poston's mining company when the Americans came in 1856. The museum showcases every culture, with artifacts and displays that bring 2,000 years of history to life. The state park is also a trailhead for the Juan Bautista De Anza Trail that leads to Tumacacori National Historical Park.

1 Burruel St, Tubac, AZ 85646
520-398-2252 • TubacPresidio.org
AZStateParks.com / NPS.gov

Warren Earp's Grave

Warren Earp, the youngest brother of Virgil, Wyatt and Morgan, is buried in the Willcox Cemetery not too far from where he was gun downed by Johnny Boyette in Brown's Saloon in 1900. After paying your respects at Warren's monument, enjoy a visit to a museum dedicated to Cochise County's very own, Rex Allen, at the Rex Allen "Arizona Cowboy" Museum & Willcox Cowboy Hall of Fame.

454 N 3rd St, Willcox, AZ
ExploreCochise.com

Yuma

Near the confluence of the Gila and Colorado rivers, the U.S. Army built a post at the strategic crossing of the Colorado. Today the Yuma Quartermaster Depot State Historic

Park provides a window into early Territorial settlement, steamboat military, railroad and mining history. Across the highway from the depot is the notorious Yuma Territorial Prison State Historic Park, once one of the most feared prisons in the Old West.

201 N 4th Ave, Yuma, AZ 85364
928-783-0071 • *VisitYuma.com*
AZStateParks.com

New Mexico

Battle of Glorieta Pass, Pecos National Historical Park

A separate unit from the main visitor center of Pecos National Historical Park, the Glorieta Battlefield commemorates the key battle between New Mexico forces and the Confederate Army that had been attempting to secure Southern control over the Southwest. To walk the park's 2.35-mile Glorieta Battlefield hiking trail, ask the rangers at the Pecos National Historical Park visitor center to provide you the gate code and a map.

NM-63, Pecos, NM 87552
505-757-7241 • *NPS.gov*

El Morro National Monument

For centuries travelers across New Mexico would cite El Morro as a key landmark on their trail north and south from the Pueblo communities along the Rio Grande and New Spain's settlements in Mexico. Many who paused and rested at the butte's watering hole carved their name into its sandstone face. With over 2,000 inscriptions, El Morro's importance from ancient times to the present is documented at the monument's visitor center and along the Inscription Trail to Inscription Rock, and the

Headland Trail to Atsinna, the 875-room pueblo ruin atop El Morro.

Ice Caves Rd, Grants, NM 87020
505-783-4226 • *NPS.gov*

Fort Bayard National Historic Landmark

Built in the territory of New Mexico east of Silver City in 1866, Fort Bayard was an army camp until 1900 when it became a military hospital. Adjacent to the former hospital (closed in 2010) is the Fort Bayard National Cemetery, opened in 1866, and operated by the Veteran's Administration. The museum is open every Monday, April through September and by appointment only, October through March.

3rd St & D Ave, Fort Bayard, NM
575-956-3294 • *FortBayard.org*
SilverCityTourism.org

Fort Selden Historic Site

Built in 1865 along the Rio Grande River in the Mesilla Valley, Fort Selden was an important Army post in the Southwestern Apache wars until its closure in 1891. Just ten miles north of Las Cruces, Fort Selden Historic Site offers a visitors center, adobe ruins visitors can walk through and on

Kit Carson Home & Museum
★Taos
● St. James Hotel
● Fort Union National Monument
Palace of the Governors ★Las Vegas
Santa Fe ⊛
● Battle of Glorieta Pass, Pecos National Historical Park
El Morro ● ★Albuquerque
National Monument
● Fort Sumner Historic Site
● Fort Stanton Historic Site
● Lincoln
● Fort Bayard National Historic Landmark
Fort Selden Historic Site ●
Las Cruces ★
● Pat Garrett Murder Site Historical Marker
Mesilla ●
Village of Columbus & Camp Furlong

weekends during summer months, living history events with re-enactors in period dress.

1233 Fort Selden Rd
Las Cruces, NM 88007 • 575-647-9585
NMHistoricSites.org

Fort Stanton Historic Site

Built in 1855, Fort Stanton was a key Territorial outpost in the Army's war with the Mescalero Apache tribe until its closure in 1896. The fort's soldiers were also called into service during local conflicts, including the Lincoln County War between Billy the Kid and his Regulators fighting for the Tunstall-McSween faction and the Murphy-Dolan faction. Just ten miles from Lincoln, visitors should start their tour at the Fort Stanton Museum before taking a walking tour of the 240-acre site, which has 88 historic buildings.

104 Kit Carson Rd
Fort Stanton, NM 88323
575-354-0341 • *NMHistoricSites.org*

Fort Sumner Historic Site/ Bosque Redondo Memorial

During the Civil War, the U.S. fought a war with the Navajo people that led to the tribe's defeat and long walk to incarceration adjacent to Fort Sumner at the Bosque Redondo Reservation. The miserable location for the 8,500 Navajos led the tribe to negotiate a peace settlement that allowed them to return with sovereignty to their traditional lands in the Four Corners region. Over 500 Mescalero Apaches who had also been incarcerated at Bosque Redondo fled the reservation in 1865. Visitors should tour the museum and walk the Old Fort Site and River Walk trails. The outlaw Billy the Kid was killed in the town of Fort Sumner on July 14, 1881, and is buried in the village cemetery.

707 N 4th St, Fort Sumner, NM 88119
575-355-7705 • *NMHistoricSites.org*

Fort Union National Monument

One of the most significant U.S. Army posts in eastern New Mexico, Fort Union was built at the crossroads of the Santa Fe Trail's Mountain and Cimarron Cut-off trails. Re-enactors hold regular events at the monument and visitors will enjoy the many tours of the grounds and the fort's well-preserved ruins.

NM 161, Ocate, NM 87734
505-425-8025 • *NPS.gov*

Kit Carson Home and Museum

Located in the center of Taos, Kit Carson's family adobe has been preserved as a museum that interprets his dramatic—and controversial—life as a mountain man, explorer, trailblazer, soldier and family man.

113 Kit Carson Rd, Taos, NM 87571
575-758-4945 • *KitCarsonMuseum.org*

Lincoln

In the annals of Western U.S. history, the humble town of Lincoln's notorious past is synonymous with the violence that plagued the West, and especially the New Mexico Territory after the Civil War. The historic buildings in the center of town are managed and preserved as a New Mexico Historic Site. Visitors can walk the streets of Lincoln and stride in the footsteps of the Regulators, Billy the Kid, Pat Garrett, John Tunstall, Alexander McSween, Lawrence G. Murphy and James J. Dolan. Stay the weekend at the Dolan House, Ellis Store or Wortley Hotel. Tour the 17 historic structures (call ahead for scheduled openings), including the Old Lincoln County Courthouse, the Tunstall Store, Montaño store, the 1850s stone Torreon, San Juan Mission Church and the Anderson-Freeman Museum. Old Lincoln Days are held every August and re-enactors entertain tourists with some of the most infamous moments of the Lincoln County War, including Billy's dramatic escape from the Lincoln County Jail.

Highway 380 Mile Marker 97.5
Lincoln, NM 88338
575-653-4025 • *NMHistoricSites.org*

Mesilla

Founded in 1848, Mesilla is one of the oldest settlements in the southern Rio Grande River Valley in New Mexico and was an important crossroads for territorial trade and travel on the El Camino Real and Southern Overland Route of the Butterfield Stage Line. Mesilla's historic plaza is where U.S. troops from Fort Fillmore raised the American flag after the conclusion of the Gadsden Purchase in 1853. The town served as the short-lived capital of the Confederacy in New Mexico during the Civil War. In the 1870s and 1880s Mesilla's popular saloons and dance halls attracted law-abiding citizens and outlaws, including Billy the Kid. Visitors should tour the historic plaza (the Kid was tried and sentenced to die in the historic building that is home to today's Billy the Kid Giftshop), the local Gadsden Museum and the New Mexico Ranch & Farm Museum in nearby Las Cruces.

2231 Avenida de Mesilla
Mesilla, NM 88046 • 575-524-3262
OldMesilla.org

Palace of the Governors

Built of adobe in the early 1600s as New Spain's seat of government in New Mexico, today it is the state's preeminent museum and archives of the city, state and region's history. A Registered National Historic Landmark and American Treasure, the Palace of the Governors is the oldest occupied public building in the United States. The New Mexico History Museum opened next door to the Palace on Santa Fe's Historic Plaza in 2009 and is dedicated to the ancient

The only known photograph of outlaw Billy the Kid was most likely taken in 1879 or 1880 in Fort Sumner, New Mexico Territory.

– TRUE WEST ARCHIVES –

multi-cultural history of the Land of Enchantment state.

105 W Palace Ave, Santa Fe, NM 87501
505 476 5100
PalaceOfTheGovernors.org
NMHistoryMuseum.org

Pat Garrett Murder Site Historical Marker

Sheriff Pat Garrett became famous for his killing of Billy the Kid, but along the way the notorious and controversial lawman made many enemies in many powerful moneyed circles in the territory of New Mexico. One morning, violence ended Garret's life, much like he lived it, and a marker commemorates his assassination in Dona Ana County.

Jornada Rd & I-70 Service Rd,
Las Cruces, NM
NMHistoricMarkers.org

Jumping over the lifeless body of Harvey Morris, Billy the Kid returns fire and dashes for the creek.

– ILLUSTRATIONS BY BOB BOZE BELL –

Billy the Kid's Backyard Ballet

July 19, 1878

Fire is licking at the last room—Susan McSween's kitchen. In this final refuge, Alexander McSween sits with his head in his hands. His 12 defenders are crowded into this crumbling, tiny space, where the walls are too hot to touch and the air is heavy with smoke. The men are blackened, tired, thirsty and desperate, but they've decided to wait until dark before attempting to escape.

Housebound for nearly five days, the 12 men in the McSween home were holding their own until around 2 p.m. today, when one member of Sheriff George Peppin's posse, Andrew Boyle, torched the northwest corner of the house.

At approximately 9 p.m., five defenders, including Billy Kid, jump into the backyard and run toward a gate in the side yard. (One report says they are not wearing their boots or shoes.) Before they reach the gate, four Peppin men along the outside of the back wall spot them and open fire.

Law student Harvey Morris is shot dead at the gate. The remaining four, including Billy Kid, leap over his body and return fire as they race for the creek. Incredibly, they make it.

McSween and another group of his besieged men make their move. But as they approach the east gate, just outside the shadow of the flames, the guns at the back gate explode, driving McSween and his men back. They stay in the corner "about five minutes" before making yet another attempt, which also sends them scurrying back into the shadows.

Gunshots and yells are heard from across the creek as the Kid and crew celebrate their hair-raising escape.

Ten grueling minutes pass. All the guns along the back wall are aimed at the darkness. Finally, McSween allegedly says, "I shall surrender."

Huddled along the back fence at the north gate are four Peppin men: Joseph Nash, Robert Beckwith, John Jones and Andrew Boyle. They are soon joined by a man known as "Dummy."

"I am a deputy sheriff and I have a warrant for your arrest," yells Beckwith, just before he opens the gate and enters the backyard. Leading the quartet into the yard, Beckwith reaches the darkened corner when someone shouts, "I shall never surrender!" and Beckwith is shot in the eye. The men behind Beckwith empty their guns into the darkness.

As fire consumes the last remaining wall in the house, six bodies lie crumpled in the backyard: Alexander McSween, Francisco Zamora, Vicente Romero, Harvey Morris, Yginio Salazar and Robert Beckwith.

The fight is over.   ★

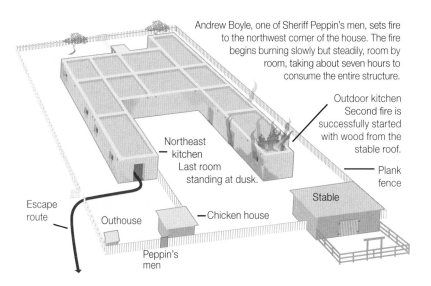

Andrew Boyle, one of Sheriff Peppin's men, sets fire to the northwest corner of the house. The fire begins burning slowly but steadily, room by room, taking about seven hours to consume the entire structure.

Outdoor kitchen
Second fire is successfully started with wood from the stable roof.

Northeast kitchen
Last room standing at dusk.

Plank fence

Escape route

Stable

Outhouse

Chicken house

Peppin's men

Robert Beckwith (right, foreground) aims into the darkness as he, Joseph Nash (second from right) and "Dummy" move in to arrest McSween. It is all a desperate ruse as Beckwith is shot dead by a bullet in the eye. You can just see the pistol barrel sticking out from the edge of the chicken house.

St. James Hotel

In Cimarron, the historic St. James Hotel bears the bullet holes in its ceiling as evidence of its Wild West past as a Lambert's Saloon before the proprietors expanded it into a popular hotel. Many well-known Westerners traveling along the Santa Fe Railway stopped for the night, including Buffalo Bill Cody, who was a friend of the owners—French chef Henri Lambert and his wife, Mary. Today, the historic hotel welcomes guests to enjoy the vintage, well-appointed rooms and a meal and drink at the restaurant and saloon.

617 S Collison, Cimarron, NM 87714
575-376-2664 • *ExStJames.com*

Village of Columbus/ Camp Furlong

On March 9, 1916, Mexican revolutionary Gen. Francisco "Pancho" Villa led a raid into the United States across the border into the Village of Columbus and past the troops stationed at Camp Furlong. With nearly 500 Villistas riding hard wantonly through the town, the revolutionaries set fire to downtown before suffering dozens of losses. Today, the only attack on U.S. soil by foreign invaders until 9/11 is remembered at Pancho Villa State Park, the former Camp Furlong from which Gen. Jack Pershing led 10,000 soldiers into Mexico in search of Villa.

224 Lima Ave, Columbus, NM 88029
575-531-0046
ColumbusNewMexico.com

Oklahoma

101 Ranch Memorial

The internationally renowned Miller Brothers' 101 Ranch Wild West Show, billed as "The Greatest Show of the West," toured the world from 1905 to 1939. During the Miller Brothers heyday, the Oklahoma family empire included vast land holdings, oil wells and international fame. The 101 Ranch Old Timers Association owns 72 acres of the original ranch site and in 1996 opened the public picnic area. Visit the E.W. Marland's Grand Home Museum in Ponca City to see the official 101 Ranch Collection and 101 Ranch Old Timers Association Museum. Visit Ponca City in June to experience the annual celebration since 1960 of the great 101 Ranch Wild West Show at the 101 Ranch Rodeo.

On State Highway 156, 13 miles SW of Ponca City • *101RanchOTA.com*
KayCounty.info
MarlandGrandHome.com

Chisholm Trail Heritage Center

In Duncan, Oklahoma, The Chisholm Trail Heritage Center is located north of the Red River along the historic Chisholm Trail. An interactive museum with regularly scheduled events inside the exhibit hall and outside on the museum's grounds, the centerpiece of the Chisholm Trail Heritage Center is

Many big outfits in the West, including New Mexico's Canjilon Ranch, turned their headquarters into dude ranches for tourists to enjoy a real, Old West experience, near Canjilon, New Mexico, circa 1925.

– EDWARD KEMP/NEW MEXICO HISTORY MUSEUM, NEGATIVE NO. 053697 –

Oklahoma rancher and 101 Ranch & Wild West Show owner, Joe Miller proudly poses on his Arab stallion Ben-Hur. Joe was the oldest of three brothers who inherited the famed Ponca City area ranch from their father George Washington Miller.

The movies show cowboys bedding down using their saddle as a pillow and the saddle blanket to lie on. The real cowboys wanted it a little bit softer. They had bags filled with feathers, down, and/or cotton. When rolled up, they were too big to carry on the backs of their horses, so they were loaded into the wagons that followed the cowboys on roundups and cattle drives.

the Garis Gallery of the American West. In addition to the museum's extraordinary Western art collection, visitors will enjoy both permanent and temporary exhibitions that celebrate the history and culture of the Chisholm Trail, American cowboy and the West. When walking the museum grounds, don't miss Paul Moore's *On the Chisholm Trail* bronze that greets visitors at the entrance to the Heritage Center.

1000 Chisholm Trail Pkwy
Duncan, OK 73533 • 580-252-6692
OnTheChisholmTrail.com

Fort Gibson Historic Site

A national historic landmark, Fort Gibson dates to 1824 when the U.S. Army began exploring the region. A key post during the Indian Removal era, it was closed in 1857. After the Civil War started the fort was reoccupied and became a key military outpost until 1890. Tours should begin at the Commissary Visitor Center on Garrison Hill and proceed through the reconstructed log fort, and historic buildings constructed between the 1840s and 1870s. Visitors also enjoy re-enactors leading living history programs and events during the year.

110 E Ash Ave, Fort Gibson, OK 74434
918-478-4088 • *OKHistory.org*

Fort Sill National Historic Landmark & Museum

One of the most significant historical military museums in Old West history, the Fort Sill National Historic Landmark and Museum is dedicated to the interpretation of nearly a century of American and Indian history in the region, including the post-Civil War engagements with the Southern Plains tribes. Fort Sill was enlarged in 1894 when the Chiricahua Indians, imprisoned for nearly a decade in Florida and Alabama, were moved permanently to a reservation at the military base. The interactive history facility boasts 38 buildings and curates over 235,000 objects at the 142-acre Historic Landmark. The museum is completely dedicated to its historic era, while the US Army Field Artillery Museum has been a separate institution since 2008.

437 Quanah Rd, Fort Sill, OK 73503
580-442-5123 • *Sill-WWW.Army.mil*

Fort Supply Historic Site

Founded out of necessity during the winter of 1868 to support the Army's war with the Southern Plains tribes in Western Oklahoma, Fort Supply was a key outpost in the Indian Territory for 25 years until its closure in 1894. Today, five original buildings, including the 1875 ordance sergeant's quarters and a replica of the 1868 stockade, can be toured at the site. Visitors should start at the restored and furnished 1892 brick guardhouse, which houses Fort Supply's exhibitions.

1 William S Key Blvd, Fort Supply, OK 73841 • 580-256-6136 • *OKHistory.org*

Fort Towson Historic Site

Built in 1824 to protect early settler in the Arkansas Territory, Fort Towson was a key border outpost between Mexico and the United States prior to the Texas Revolution. The Choctaw and Chickasaw encamped at the fort before settlement in the Indian Territory. U.S. forces prepared for war against Mexico at the fort in 1846 before it was closed in 1856. The Confederate Army had its headquarters at the abandoned fort and in 1865 the final Southern surrender, by Gen. Stand Watie, occurred at Fort Towson. Visitors can tour the Suttler's Store, 18 interpretive sites on a walking tour, and enjoy regularly

scheduled living history demonstrations throughout the year.

896 N 4375 Rd, Fort Towson, OK 74735 580-873-2634 • *OKHistory.org*

Honey Springs Battlefield Historic Site

North of Checotah and adjacent to Rentiesville, the Honey Springs Battlefield Historic Site commemorates and honors the largest of 107 engagements in the Indian Territory during the Civil War. Visitors can walk six different trails across the 1,100-acre park and learn about the July 17, 1863 Battle of Honey Springs at 55 interpretive sites. The Union's decisive defeat of the Confederate forces has earned the battle the nickname "Gettysburg of the Indian Territory." A new visitor center is under construction in Rentiesville.

101601 S 4232 Rd, Checotah, OK 74426 918-473-5572 • *OKHistory.org*

On November 27, 1868, Lt. Col. George A. Custer led the U.S. 7th Cavalry surprise attack on the Southern Cheyenne village of Peace Chief Black Kettle, after which he marched them in the snow to Camp Supply. Today, the battle is commemorated at the Washita Battlefield National Historic Site.

– TRUE WEST ARCHIVES –

National Cowboy Western & Heritage Museum

Founded in 1955 in Oklahoma's capital city, the National Cowboy Hall of Fame and Museum is one of the preeminent museums in the United States dedicated to the cultural history and heritage of the American West. Annually more than 10 million visitors tour its Western art galleries, Old West and American Indian history galleries, and its three halls of fame: the Hall of Great Westerners, Hall of Great Western Performers and Rodeo Hall of Fame.

1700 NE 63rd St
Oklahoma City, OK 73111
405-478-2250
NationalCowboyMuseum.org

Oklahoma Territorial Museum

In Guthrie, the Oklahoma Territorial Museum and Carnegie Library is the centerpiece of the historic downtown district that honors and celebrates the Oklahoma's transformation from Indian Territory to statehood that began with the 1889 land run. The downtown district is on the Register of Historic Places and is the largest contiguous urban historic district in the country. Begin your tour of the Guthrie Museum Complex in the museum at the Territorial and first state capital building before taking a walking tour of the historic city.

406 E Oklahoma Ave, Guthrie, OK 73044
405-282-1889 • *OKTerritorialMuseum.org*

Washita Battlefield National Historic Site

The Lt. Col. George A. Custer-led U.S. 7th Cavalry surprise attack at dawn on the Southern Cheyenne village of Peace Chief Black Kettle on November 27, 1868, is commemorated at the Washita Battlefield National Historic Site. Follow the 1.5-mile trail from the overlook to the site of Black Kettle's village and learn

about the tragic conflict between the U.S. and the Southern Plains Indian tribes.

426 E Broadway, Cheyenne, OK 73628
580-497-2742 • *NPS.gov*

Texas

The Alamo

Internationally the most recognized historical site in the state of Texas, the Alamo is a Shrine of Texas Liberty and those who visit should revere it as hallowed ground. Built originally by Spanish pioneers in 1718, the Mission San Antonio de Valero was abandoned in the 1790s. By 1836 and the Texas War of Independence, the mission was known best by its nickname "El Alamo" renamed by Spanish soldiers in the early 1800s. Visitors to the Alamo will enjoy the various tour opportunities of the mission and battlefield site, history talks, audio tours, regularly scheduled special events and the unique Phil Collins Collection of Alamo and Texas history.

300 Alamo Plaza, San Antonio, TX 78205
210-225-1391 • *TheAlamo.org*

Concordia Cemetery

Take a walk back into time in El Paso's historic Concordia Cemetery, the eternal resting place for the famous and infamous, valiant and brave, humble and unknown. El Pasoans have buried their dead in the graveyard since the first soul was interred in the 1840s. The historic cemetery is managed by the Concordia Heritage Association to protect, preserve and maintain the graveyard. Visitors can walk its grounds and see outlaw John Wesley Hardin's grave as well as the grave of John Selman, the lawman who put Hardin in Concordia. Don't miss the special section dedicated to Buffalo Soldiers, the graves of Texas Rangers, Civil War veterans and the innumerable headstones of El Paso's citizenry forgotten with time.

3700 E Yandell Dr, El Paso, TX 79903
915-842-8200 • *ConcordiaCemetery.org*

Map of Texas showing locations:
- First Battle of Adobe Walls Site Historic Marker
- Second Battle of Adobe Walls-Battle Ground Marker
- ★ Amarillo
- Palo Duro Canyon State Park
- ★ Lubbock
- Fort Worth Stockyards National Historic District
- ★ Dallas-Fort Worth
- Concordia Cemetery
- ★ El Paso
- Fort Concho National Historic Landmark
- Waco Suspension Bridge
- San Elizario Historic District
- Enchanted Rock State Natural Area
- Old Fort Parker Historic Site
- Hueco Tanks State Park & Historic Site
- Historic Fort Stockton
- ⊛ Austin
- Fort Davis National Historic Site
- San Jacinto Battle Monument
- The Alamo
- ★ San Antonio
- Houston ★
- San Antonio Missions National Historical Park
- Enchanted Rock State Natural Area
- Goliad State Park & Goliad Historic Site
- Palo Alto Battlefield National Historic Monument

Enchanted Rock State Natural Area

An ancient dome of granite in Texas's Hill Country, Enchanted Rock has been a landmark to the peoples of the region for thousands of years. Protected in a state natural area, the landmark 425-fott pink granite outcropping, has over 400 archeological sites, and is considered sacred by many tribes. Enchanted Rock was the site of a famous shootout between Texas Ranger Capt. Jack Hays and a band of Comanches in 1841. Today, visitors can hike its trails, explore the granite dome and star-gaze, all the while considering why the local Tonkawa believed the granite dome was the "Glowing, singing rock."

16710 Ranch Rd 965
Fredericksburg, TX 78624
830-685-3636 • TPWD.State.Tx.gov

First Battle of Adobe Walls Site Historic Marker and Second Battle of Adobe Walls-Battle Ground Marker

Southern Plains pioneer and proprietor William Bent built an adobe trading post on Bent Creek north of the Canadian River in 1843. Five years after his initial log cabin was expanded into an adobe fort he closed and blew up his 80-square-foot outpost because of Indian attacks. In November 1864 and then in June 1874, the ruins of Bent's adobe fort became ingrained in Western history as the site of the First and Second Battle of Adobe Walls, respectively. Visit the Hutchison County

At the age of nine, Quanah Parker, the eldest of Comanche father Peta Nocona and white mother Cynthia Parker's three children, lost his mother when she was taken by the Texas Rangers in 1860. In 1884, Quanah ran a newspaper advertisement in search of a photo of his mother, who had died before he could reunite with her. A.F. Corning, who took a daguerreotype of Cynthia with Quanah's sister in 1862, responded. Quanah, at last, had a photo of his mother.

– COURTESY COWAN'S AUCTIONS, DECEMBER 9, 2009 –

Historical Museum in Borger to learn more about the local history, culture and the two Battles of Adobe Walls.

613 N Main, Borger, TX 79008
806-274-2211 • *BorgerChamber.org*

Fort Concho
National Historic Landmark

Built in 1867 as a strategic U.S. Army outpost during the post-Civil War conflict with the Southern Plains tribes, Fort Concho served its purpose effectively until it was closed in 1889. The City of San Angelo operates the historic landmark, museum and the staffing and preservation of 23 fort buildings. Walk in the footsteps of soldiers and their families who lived at the fort and tour Officers Row and Quarters, the Enlisted Men's Barracks, Post Headquarters, Hospital, School House and Chapel. Fort Concho is also the site of numerous annual living history events, including Buffalo Soldier Heritage Day in February and Fort Concho Frontier Day in April.

630 S Oakes St, San Angelo, TX 76903
325-481-2646 • *FortConcho.com*

Fort Davis
National Historic Site

From 1854 to 1891, Fort Davis played a strategic military role in the settlement of West Texas and the protection of travelers on the San Antonio-El Paso Road. Today, Fort Davis National Historic Site is one of the best examples of frontier posts involved with the Indian Wars with the Comanche, Apache and Kiowa people in the American Southwest. Visitors can tour the fort's restored and refurnished buildings on a self-guided tour, and enjoy regular scheduled living history events with re-enactors in period and military dress, including an annual Independence Day celebration.

101 Lt. Henry Flipper Dr, Fort Davis, TX 79734 • 432-426-3224 • *NPS.gov*

Fort Worth Stockyards
National Historic District

From 1866 to 1890, Texas cowboys drove the cattle north to market, and in the early days, Fort Worth was a last stop before the trail boss headed his outfit and herd north across the Red River, across Oklahoma to the rail heads in Kansas. After the railroad arrived in 1876, Fort Worth became a shipping station and the first stockyards were built. For the next seven decades, Fort Worth developed into the nation's largest stockyard and livestock exchange in the nation. In the 1970s, with the steady decline in the cattle business and packing houses in the city, the Fort Worth Historical Society was created to preserve the historic district. Today, the Fort Worth Stockyards National Historic District is one of the most visited tourist attractions in the state (don't miss the twice-a-day longhorn cattle drives), and cattle are still sold at the Livestock Exchange Building every week—via satellite.

131 E. Exchange Ave
Suite 110
Fort Worth, TX 76164
817-625-5082
StockyardsMuseum.org

Goliad State Park & Goliad Historic Site

When visitors arrive at Goliad State Park they should be prepared to take a walk into Spanish Colonial, Mexican and Texan history. Tour a 1930s refurnished restoration of the Spanish Colonial Era Mission of Nuestra Señora del Espíritu Santo de Zuñiga, the reconstructed birthplace of Mexican Cinco de Mayo hero General Ignacio Zaragoza, the Fannin Memorial Monument and the 1749 Presidio La Bahia, where Fannin and his men were executed under the orders of Mexican Gen. Santa Ana in 1836. The Fannin Battleground State Historic Site is ten miles east of Goliad, and well worth a tour, as is a walk through Goliad's historic downtown.

108 Park Rd 6, Goliad, TX 77963
361-645-3405 • *TPWD.State.Tx.gov*

Historic Fort Stockton

First constructed in 1856 near present-day Pecos, Camp Stockton was abandoned in 1861 at the outbreak of the Civil War. In 1867, Fort Stockton was re-established at its current location and

The bespectacled cowboy models the best gear he owns from his hat to his spurs, including his wild rag, fringed shotgun chaps, leather wrist cuffs and grass rope.

– TRUE WEST ARCHIVES –

garrisoned with the 9th Cavalry, a newly created Black regiment. The fort was used to the tactical advantage of the Army in its fight with Southern Plains Indian tribes until it was closed in 1886. Historic Fort Stockton consists today of the parade ground, the guard house, two reconstructed enlisted men's barracks and kitchens, and three structures from the original Officers' Row, two of which are open to the public.

301 E. 3rd St, Fort Stockton, TX 79735
432-336-2400 • *HistoricFortStockton.org*

Hueco Tanks State Park and Historic Site

Home to ancient peoples long before the Spanish entrada into the region, modern Indian tribes found refuge, water and shelter amidst the tanks, as did succeeding generations of explorers, travelers, settlers, and even the Butterfield Overland Mail had a station there in the late 1850s. A

The earliest known photograph of the Alamo, this daguerreotype was taken before 1850. Historians estimate approximately 2,300 Mexican soldados attacked the mission during the 13-day siege in 1836 that killed, almost to the man, the roughly 250 Texian defenders.

– COURTESY DOLPH BRISCOE CENTER FOR AMERICAN HISTORY, UNIVERSITY OF TEXAS AT AUSTIN –

working ranch from the 1890s to the 1940s, the rancher's adobe home is the park's interpretive center today.

6900 Hueco Ranks Rd No. 1
El Paso, TX 79938 • 915-857-1135
TPWD.State.TX.us

Old Fort Parker Historic Site

Fort Parker bears the name of the family who suffered an Indian raid on May 19, 1836, that led to the kidnapping of nine-year-old Cynthia Parker. She would be raised as a Comanche and married to Chief Peta Nocona. Their son grew up to be the legendary Chief Quanah Parker, the last to lead the Comanches in war on the Southern Plains. Tour the restored fort, built in 1936 in honor of the Texas Centennial, adjacent to Fort Parker State Park.

866 Park Rd 35
Groesbeck, TX 76642
254-729-5253
OldFortParker.org

Palo Alto Battlefield National Historic Monument

On May 8, 1846, the Mexican American War started on on the prairie of Palo Alto near the Gulf of Mexico. Visitors to the Palo Alto Battlefield Historic Monument should begin their tour at the visitor center's museum before walking interpretive trails to the battlefield site.

7200 Paredes Line Rd
Brownsville, TX 78526
956-541-2785 • *NPS.gov*

Palo Duro Canyon State Park

In the Panhandle of Texas, Paul Duro Canyon State Park, known as "The Grand Canyon of Texas," protects a unique natural and culturally important site in the Lone Star state. Home to Native peoples for over 12,000 years, the Comanche and Kiowa tribes occupied the canyon

El Paso's Concordia Cemetery is the final resting place for 60,000 souls including notorius gunman John Wesley Hardin, whose grave is well-protected and frequently visited.

lands prior to their wars with the U.S. in the 19th century. In 1874, the tribes suffered a major defeat in a battle at Palo Duro, and two years later, famous cattle baron Charles Goodnight established his JA Ranch in the canyon. Events are held at the park every month, but for five decades *Texas! Outdoor Musical* held in the Pioneer Amphitheatre in the Canyon, June to Mid-August, is the highlight of the year.

11450 State Hwy Park Rd 5
Canyon, TX 79015
806-488-2227 • *TPWD.Texas.gov*

San Antonio Missions National Historical Park

A World Heritage Site since 2015 that includes the Alamo, San Antonio Missions National Historical Park protects, preserves and interprets Missions Concepción, San José, San Juan and Espada, four of the most important 18th century Spanish Mission complexes in North America.

6701 San Jose Dr, San Antonio, TX 78214
210-534-1540 • *NPS.gov*

San Elizario Historic District

Just east of El Paso, the San Elizario Historic District is a living history center that provides visitors with a window into 18th and 19th century life along the Rio Grande River in southwestern Texas. Founded in 1789, the town of San Elizario grew up in support of the Presidio San Elcear. Visit the city's historic sites on a walking tour that includes the Presidio, Old City Jail, Memorial Placita and Los Portales, home to the city's museum and visitor center.

12710 Church St, San Elizario, TX 79849
915-974-7037 • *CityofSanElizario.com*

The San Jacinto Battle Monument and Museum of History annually hosts the San Jacinto Day Festival and Battle Re-enactment the third weekend of every April.

San Jacinto Battle Monument

General Sam Houston's decisive victory over Mexican leader General Santa Ana's army on April 21, 1836, is honored and enshrined at the San Jacinto Battle Monument and Museum just 20 minutes outside of Houston. The 567.31-foot obelisk towers over the battlefield site with an observation tower at the top and the San Jacinto Museum in the base. Tour the museum's exhibits and watch the film *Texas Forever!!*

1 Monument Cir, La Porte, TX 77571
281-479-2421 • *TPWD.Texas.gov*

Waco Suspension Bridge

Driving the longhorn herds north from southern Texas to Kansas, the range bosses and cowboy crews faced innumerable daily dangers, but pushing thousands of steers across rivers on the Chisholm trail led to many drownings of men and animals. The Brazos River in Waco was unpredicable, and the ferry crossing cumbersome for cattle drives. The city recognized an opportunity for the future and built a 475-foot suspension bridge, the first ever in Texas. Today, the Waco Suspension Bridge is for pedestrians only, but Waco still holds its Independence Day celebration at the bridge and Indian Springs Park, the original townsite.

Waco Visitor Information Center
106 Texas Ranger Trail, Waco, TX 76706
800-922-6386 • *WacoHeartOfTexas.com* ★

The Comanche, who once controlled a wide-swath of the Plains from Colorado to Mexico, surrendered to U.S. Army in 1874, unable to overcome the onslaught of the American expansion into the West—and the destruction of the once vast buffalo herds that were the life-blood of the Comanche people.

– TRUE WEST ARCHIVES –

Great Books

Empire of the Summer Moon: Quanah Parker and the Rise and Fall of the Comanches, the Most Powerful Indian Tribe in American History *by S.C. Gywnn* (Scribner, 2010)

Fighting for Uncle Sam: Buffalo Soldiers in the Frontier Army *by John Langellier* (Schiffer Military History, 2016)

Lonesome Dove *by Larry McMurtry* (Simon & Schuster, 1985)

Print the Legend: The Life and Times of John Ford *by Scott Eyman* (Simon & Schuster, 1999)

Texas Ranger: The Epic Life of Frank Hamer, the Man Who Killed Bonnie and Clyde *by John Boessenecker* (Thomas Dunne Books, 2016)

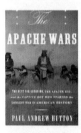

The Apache Wars: The Hunt for Geronimo, the Apache Kid, and the Captive Boy Who Started the Longest War in American History *by Paul Andrew Hutton* (Crown, 2016)

The Searchers: The Making of a Legend *by Glenn Frankel* (Bloomsbury, 2013)

The Texas Rangers: Wearing the Cinco Peso,1821-1900 *by Mike Cox* (Forge, 2009)

To Hell on a Fast Horse: The Untold Story of Billy the Kid and Pat Garrett *by Mark Lee Gardner* (William Morrow, 2010)

Tom Jeffords: Friend of Cochise *by Doug Hocking* (TwoDot, 2017)

Wyatt Earp: The Life Behind the Legend *by Casey Tefertiller* (MJF Books, 1997)

KURT RUSSELL   VAL KILMER

JUSTICE IS COMING

TOMBSTONE

Every town has a story. Tombstone has a legend.

– COURTESY BUENA VISTA PICTURES –

Western Film & TV

3:10 to Yuma (*Columbia, 1957*)

The Alamo (*United Artists, 1960*)

Arizona (*Columbia, 1940*)

Gunfight at the O.K. Corral (*Paramount, 1957*)

Life & Legend of Wyatt Earp (*ABC, 1955-1961*)

Lonesome Dove (*CBS, 1989*)

My Darling Clementine (*20th Century Fox, 1946*)

Pat Garrett & Billy The Kid (*MGM, 1973*)

Red River (*United Artists, 1948*)

The Searchers (*Warner Bros., 1956*)

The Wild Bunch (*Warner Bros., 1969*)

Tombstone (*Buena Vista Pictures, 1993*)

Winchester '73 (*Universal, 1950*)

Wyatt Earp (*Warner Bros., 1994*)

Shoot-out in El Paso

April 14, 1881

Out in the West Texas town of El Paso, ex-Marshal George Campbell is flat-out looking for trouble. "Any American that is a friend of Mexicans," he booms, "ought to be hanged!"

Constable Gus Krempkau turns red. He has just finished assisting a group of Mexicans into the U.S. "George," says Krempkau, as he slides his rifle into the scabbard aboard his riding mule, "I hope you don't mean me."

"If the shoe fits," hoots Campbell, snapping his fingers in the air for emphasis, "then wear it." A drunk Campbell then turns to grab the reins of his mule, which are tied to a tree.

Another drunk bystander, Johnny Hale, steps forward and bellows, "Turn loose,

Dallas Stoudenmire, all six feet, four inches of him, is known as "Big Dal," and he is an efficient officer, when sober. Unfortunately, as time goes on, he becomes increasingly erratic and vicious.

– PHOTOS IN "SHOOT-OUT IN EL PASO" COURTESY ROBERT G. MCCUBBIN COLLECTION –

Campbell, I've got him covered." Hale instantly fires, and the bullet hits Krempkau near the heart, before exiting through his lungs.

Across the street, the Globe Restaurant doors blow open, and Marshal Dallas Stoudenmire emerges with a pistol in each hand. Close behind him is his brother-in-law, Doc Cummings, toting a shotgun. As he takes in the scene on the fly, Stoudenmire steps lively into the street and snaps off a quick shot at Hale, who ducks behind an adobe pillar. Unfortunately, the marshal's shot misses Hale and hits a Mexican citizen who has just bought a sack of peanuts. Hale pokes his head around the pillar. Stoudenmire's second shot hits him in the head; he collapses, dead.

Drawing his own pistol, Campbell hastily backs into the center of the street and loudly says, "Gentlemen, this is not my fight."

A dying Krempkau grits his teeth and squeezes off shots at Campbell. The first bullet smashes into the ex-marshal's pistol and breaks his wrist. Campbell yells out and drops to the ground to pick up his revolver. Krempkau's next bullet hits Campbell in the foot.

Defending his mortally wounded constable, Stoudenmire fires at Campbell. The bullet enters Campbell's stomach, causing him to drop his gun a second time, as he topples face-down.

When Stoudenmire rolls Campbell over, Campbell sputters, "You big son-of-a-bitch, you murdered me!"

The fight is over.

George W. Campbell, standing next to Jim Manning, in 1881.
Campbell hailed from Kentucky and served as El Paso's deputy sheriff and city
marshal, but he quit when the town council refused to pay him. The forward butt
on his holstered pistol causes some to speculate that George was left-handed,
but testimony indicated he was right-handed.

El Paso, Texas, April 14, 1881

At 6 p.m., Marshal Dallas Stoudenmire (center) hears gunshots and exits the Globe Restaurant. Sizing up the scene, he attacks Hale and Campbell, who he assumes killed his constable, but he ends up killing an innocent bystander. Doc Cummings (far right), Dallas' brother-in-law and the owner of the Globe, steps off the sidewalk with a shotgun. He fires no shots. Backing into the middle of the street, Campbell (far left) tells them, "Gentlemen, this is not my fight."

The west side of El Paso Street, looking south. The site of the El Paso shoot-out is in the far left corner, beyond the wagon that is unloading in front of the Manning Saloon. The wagon is also near where Stoudenmire will be killed in September 1882, a mere 17 months after he gunned down ex-Marshal Campbell dead. One of the bullets fired in that gunfight will hit the barber pole to the wagon's right.

★ Stoudenmire
● Campbell
☆ Krempkau
● Hale
● Perez (bystander)
✹ Rangers

Source: Conklin map, November 1881.

The Union Pacific Railroad's ambition to serve the mining town of Leadville led the powerful rail company to found the Georgetown, Breckinridge & Leadville Railway and build the engineering wonder known as the Georgetown Loop in 1881.

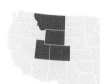

Great Basin and Rocky Mountains

Colorado, Montana, Utah and Wyoming

When William F. Cody died in Denver, Colorado, in 1917, they say he requested to be buried high on Lookout Mountain, west of the city, so that he could eternally see both the plains and mountains he loved. From Montana's snow-covered peaks to the labyrinth of canyons in Southern Utah, from Wyoming's Yellowstone country to Colorado's Continental Divide, the Great Basin and Rocky Mountains region was home to many Indian tribes before Europeans arrived in search of furs. The abundant natural resources of the region drove the conquest and settlement of the four states through the 19th century—and even continues today. Travelers in search of the Old West in the region will discover why distance is relative to the time needed to cross over high mountain passes and sagebrush deserts on foot, horseback or wagon, by transcontinental train, or in a car on ribbons of historic highways under a seemingly endless blue sky.

Yellowstone National Park, Wyoming
– COURTESY LIBRARY OF CONGRESS –

William F. "Buffalo Bill" Cody is considered the greatest promoter of the real and imagined West. The Buffalo Bill Center of the West's Buffalo Bill Museum in Cody, Wyoming, and Buffalo Bill's Grave & Museum in Golden, Colorado, are the best places to learn about Cody's influence on the history of the West since his passing in 1917.

– COURTESY BUFFALO BILL MUSEUM AND GRAVE, GOLDEN, COLORADO –

Colorado

Bent's Old Fort National Historic Site

Entrepreneurism and courage were the touchstones of William and Charles Bent who in 1833 built their trading post with their partner, Ceran St. Vrain, along the Santa Fe Trail on the north banks of the Arkansas River in the middle of Indian country. For 16 years, Bent's Fort was the "castle of the plains," and was the most important economic center between Kansas City and Santa Fe until it was abandoned in 1849. The fort was reconstructed for America's bicentennial, and serves as an active living history center.

35110 Colorado Hwy 194 East
La Junta, CO 81050
719-383-5010 • *NPS.gov*

Buffalo Bill's Grave and Museum

In Golden, Colorado, high on Lookout Mountain is William F. "Buffalo Bill" Cody's final resting place. The Western showman died while visiting his sister in Denver in 1917. His wife, Louisa, was buried next to him four years later and that same year Cody's friend, Johnny Baker, started the Buffalo Bill Memorial Museum. Today the Buffalo Bill Museum and Grave is one of the most visited historic sites in Colorado, a true testament to the lasting importance of the beloved Western showman.

987½ Lookout Mountain Rd
Golden, CO 80401
303-526-0744
BuffaloBill.org

Durango

Located in the heart of the San Juan Mountains on the banks of the Animas River in Southwest Colorado, Durango is home to the world-famous Durango-Silverton Narrow Gauge Railroad. Visitors who love Victorian inns will enjoy staying at the Historic Strater Hotel in the downtown district before taking a round-trip ride into history on the narrow-gauge railroad to Silverton and back. The train runs year 'round, with special excursions in the heart of winter.

802 Main St, Durango, CO 81302
800-463-8726 • *Durango.org*

Fort Garland Museum & Cultural Center

Built in Colorado's San Luis Valley in 1858, Fort Garland was an early outpost in the heart of the state when settlers began expanding their communities into the rich interior valleys. A key military outpost until 1883, the fort was under the command of Kit Carson in 1866-'67 because of his knowledge of the region and relationship with the local Utes. Today's visitors will enjoy the rich heritage preserved at the fort, including regularly scheduled re-enactments and living history events.

29477 Colorado Hwy 159
Fort Garland, CO 81133
719-379-3512 • *HistoryColorado.org*
MuseumTrail.org

Yellow Wolf was a Nez Perce warrior who fought with Chief Joseph in the 1877 Nez Perce War, including the final battle at Bear Paw. Today, Joseph's famous surrender site is part of the Nez Perce National Historical Park.

– COURTESY LIBRARY OF CONGRESS –

Georgetown Loop Railroad and Mining Tours

Historic Georgetown's business district is an enjoyable and informative place to begin a tour of the mining town known as the Silver Queen of the Rockies, built on the silver boom of the 1880s. The Georgetown Loop Railroad & Mining Tours is an engineering marvel and provides today's passengers views of the Clear Creek Canyon and the Rocky Mountains. For an additional fee, passengers may take a guided tour of one of three mines.

646 Loop Dr
Georgetown, CO 80444
888-456-6777
GeorgetownLooprRR.com
Georgetown-Colorado.org

Leadville

At 10,430 feet, historic Leadville, the highest incorporated city in the United States, is a mining boomtown built near the headwaters of the Arkansas River. Abe Lee discovered gold in 1860, which was followed by a silver boom in the 1870s. Start your tour at the National Mining Hall of Fame & Museum, then take the historic walking tour before boarding the popular vintage Leadville Train. Stay at the 1886 Delaware Hotel in Leadville's historic district.

Leadville/Lake County Chamber
809 Harrison Ave, Leadville, CO 80461
719-486-3900 • *Leadville.com*

Fort Vasquez Museum

In 1835, fur traders Louis Vasquez and Andrew Sublette built Fort Vasquez about 35 miles north of modern Denver. The adobe outpost was a busy site with many famous mountain men working for the frontier entrepreneurs. Near Platteville, the museum inside the re-created fort rebuilt in the 1930s, has displays and exhibits on the fur trade, mountain men, Plains Indians and frontier life.

13412 U.S. Hwy 85, Platteville, CO 80651
970-785-2832 • *HistoryColorado.org*

The Weld Council, held on Sept. 28, 1864, at Camp Weld, Denver, Colorado Territory, failed to bring peace between the American settles and Southern Plains tribes, resulting in the tragedy of the Sand Creek Massacre. Standing left to right: Unidentified, Dexter Colley (son of Agent Samuel Colley), John S. Smith, Heap of Buffalo, Bosse, sheriff and mayor Amos Steck, Unidentified soldier. Seated left to right: White Antelope, Bull Bear, Black Kettle, Neva, Na-ta-Nee (Knock Knee). Kneeling left to right: Major Edward W. Wynkoop, Captain Silas Soule

– COURTESY COLORADO HISTORICAL SOCIETY –

Sand Creek Massacre National Historic Site

Sand Creek Massacre National Historic Site is a solemn site. The park is dedicated to remembering the tragic and unforgivable attack on Chiefs Black Kettle, White Antelope and Left Hand's peaceful villages on November 29, 1864. Led by Col. John Chivington, 675 cavalrymen attacked at dawn, slaughtering 230 Cheyenne and Arapaho women, children, warriors and elderly. Visitors should plan to attend an interpretive program and take the short walk out to the monument and overlook.

County Rd 54 & County Rd W
(Near Eads), CO 81036-0249
719-438-5916 • NPS.gov

Silverton

Gold and silver were found in 1860, but miners didn't return to the Animas River Canyon to seek their fortunes until after the Civil War. In 1874, the town of Silverton was laid out and the boom was on. In 1882, the Denver & Rio Grande Railroad reached Silverton. At its height, over 2,000 called Silverton home, with more than 400 buildings, including 29 saloons. Today, historic Silverton is a popular tourist destination and the terminus of the internationally acclaimed Durango-Silverton Narrow Gauge Railroad.

414 Greene St, Silverton, CO 81433
800-752-4494 • SilvertonColorado.com

Montana

Bannack State Park

When prospector John White found gold on Grasshopper Creek in 1862, the news of the discovery created a rush to Bannack, which in 1864 became the first Territorial capital of Montana. Mining remained an important industry in Bannack until the 1930s, and in the 1950s, Montana made the historic community a state park. Today visitors step back in time and can walk through most of the 60 historic structures. Don't miss Bannack Days, held the third weekend of every July, which celebrates the early decades of the Montana Territory.

4200 Bannack Rd, Dillon, MT 59725
406-834-3413 • Bannack.org

Bear Paw Battlefield

Commemorating the final battle of the Nez Perce War of 1877, Bear Paw Battlefield is the site of Chief Joseph's famous statement, "From where the sun now stands, I will fight no more forever." Begin your tour at the Blaine County Museum in Chinook, 15 miles south of the battlefield. Call for hours of operation. Bear Paw Battlefield's

Glacier National Park

Bear Paw Battlefield

Fort Benton
Great Falls

★ **Missoula**

◉ **Helena**

Big Hole National Battlefield

★ **Bozeman**

★ **Billings**

Virginia City

Bannack State Park

Little Big Horn Battlefield
National Monument

self-guided 1¼-mile moderately difficult interpretive trail is open to the public every day during daylight hours.

15 miles south of Chinook, MT
on Highway 240
406-357-3130 • *NPS.gov*
BlaineCountyMuseum.com

Big Hole National Battlefield

Near Wisdom, Big Hole National Battlefield is a unit of the Nez Perce National Historical Park and one of the most significant sites of the Nez Perce War of 1877. An extensive museum in the visitor center displays rare artifacts and detailed exhibitions on the tragic results of the battle. Three self-guided trails take visitors onto the battlefield, to the village site and up onto the ridgeline where Col. John Gibbon's soldiers retreated and held out under duress from a Nez Perce siege while the tribe buried its dead and escaped.

16425 Hwy 43 W, Wisdom, MT 59761
406-689-3155 • *NPS.gov*

Fort Benton

Fort Benton on the Missouri River is a crossroads of history. Visitors should stay a while in the national historic landmark, the terminus of three major trails and a key stop on the Lewis and Clark and Nez Perce National Historic trails. Museum lovers will enjoy Historic Old Fort Benton, the Museum of the

Upper Missouri, Museum of the Northern Great Plains, the Missouri River Breaks Interpretive Center, the Historic District and Levee Walk, the Shep Memorial and the State of Montana's Lewis and Clark Memorial.

U.S. Hwy 87, 40 miles northeast of Great Falls or 72 miles south of Havre, MT
406-622-3864 • *FortBenton.com*

Great Falls

Upriver from Fort Benton, the Lewis and Clark National Historic Trail leads to Great Falls, a key stop for heritage travelers to view and tour the site of the Corps of Discovery's portage of the five waterfalls on the Missouri River. Travelers should visit the C.M. Russell Museum, Giant Springs State Park and the Lewis and Clark Interpretive Center and enjoy a short or long walk, run or bike ride on the 48-mile River's Edge Trail.

1106 9th St South, Great Falls, MT 59405
406-771-1180 • *GenuineMontana.com*

Glacier National Park

Known as the Crown of the Continent, Glacier National Park was a traditional homeland to Native Blackfeet, Kootnei, Pend d'Oreillie and Salish tribes. With the Blackfeet controlling the region into the 1870s, American settlers were slow to homestead the area, but with the arrival of the Great Northern Railroad in 1891, homesteading and prospecting increased pressure on the natural beauty of the area. Tourism became a source of income, and with the rise of the national park movement, President William H. Taft made Glacier the 10th national park in 1910.

64 Grinnell Dr, West Glacier, MT 59936
406-888-7800 • *NPS.gov*

Little Bighorn Battlefield National Monument

Little Bighorn remains one of most significant battles in American history. Located on the Crow Agency, the June 25-26, 1876, battle between Sitting Bull and Crazy Horse's Sioux and Cheyenne allies and Lt. Col. George A. Custer's 7th Cavalry, led to the death of 263 soldiers, including Custer. Visitors will discover a solemnity that imbues the park, whether one is touring the national cemetery, the visitor center museum, the walkways, the 1881 7th Cavalry Memorial or the 2003 Indian Memorial. Ranger-led programs provide expert analysis on the battle, while a drive out to the Benteen-Reno Battlefield provides a great view of the Little Bighorn River Valley. After

touring the monument, don't miss an opportunity to visit the Custer Battlefield Museum, in Garryowen, Montana, or a chance to stay the night at the fully restored, historic Sheridan Inn in Sheridan, Wyoming.

756 Battlefield Tour Rd, Crow Agency, MT 59022 406-638-3224
NPS.gov / CusterMuseum.org
SheridanInn.com

Virginia City

In 1863, prospectors looking for the next bonanza discovered gold in Alder Gulch. Soon Virginia City was the latest Western boomtown that brought settlers deep into the Northern Plains. Within a year, 8,000 to 10,000 miners were living in the wild town. Soon thereafter Virginia City was made the Territorial capital. Today, visitors can walk the historic streets of the Victorian mining town, tour several historic structures, be entertained by re-enactors, take a ride on a train and learn how Virginia City, Montana, changed the course of history in the West.

800-829-2969 • *VirginiaCity.com*

The Indian Memorial at Little Bighorn Battlefield National Monument was dedicated June 25, 2014, at the 138th anniversary of the battle. The site of the monument has a 360-degree view of the battlefield and honors all the Indian tribes that fought on both sides of the conflict.

– COURTESY MONTANA OFFICE OF TOURISM AND BUSINESS DEVELOPMENT –

Utah

Bluff Fort

In 1879-'80 Mormon pioneers built a 250-mile trail from Parowan to Bluff that remains symbolic of the determination of the missionaries and their loyalty to themselves and the Church of Jesus Christ of Latter-day Saints. Soon after the pioneers settled along the San Juan River they built Bluff Fort and moved the community members into cabins inside the fort to protect them from Indian attacks. Visitors can tour a replica of the fort, an original cabin, and replicas of other buildings, including the Co-op Store, which now serves as the visitors center and gift shop.

550 Black Locust Ave, Bluff, UT 84512
435-672-9995 • *BluffUtah.org*
HIRF.org

Fort Douglas Military Museum

The Army post was built in 1862 just east of Salt Lake City to guard the Central Overland Route. In the early years, soldiers at Camp Douglas played an important peacekeeping role in the region and served to protect the construction of the transcontinental railroad in 1869. The fort served the regular Army until 1991, although the Army Reserve still maintains a 51-acre site. Today, visitors can enjoy the Fort Douglas Military Museum on the campus of the University of Utah.

32 Potter St, Salt Lake City, UT 84113
801-581-1251 • *FortDouglas.org*

Golden Spike National Historic Site

On May 10, 1869, the Central Pacific and Union Pacific railroads completed the engineering feat of the first transcontinental railroad in North America at Promontory Summit, Utah Territory. Today, the Golden Spike National Historic Site protects, interprets and promotes the memorable moment with visitor center exhibitions and film, interpretive hiking and walking trails, and living history re-enactments, including a regular re-enactment of the meeting of the two steam locomotives *Jupiter* and *No. 119* nose-to-nose, and the driving of the Golden Spike.

6450 N 22000 W, Corinne, UT 84307
435-471-2209 • *NPS.gov*

Goulding's Trading Post

In the early 1920s, sheep trader Harry Goulding and his wife, Leone, known to all as "Mike," came to Monument Valley and started a trading post. During the Depression, Harry and "Mike" went to Hollywood with photographs of their beautiful valley to drum up business for the impoverished area, and John Ford agreed it was perfect for his upcoming film, *Stagecoach*. Ever since, Monument Valley has been a favorite location for movie companies, and Goulding's quickly became Ford's headquarters in

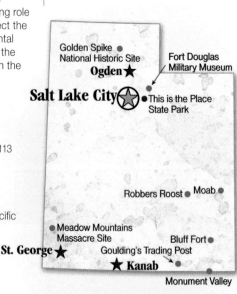

The Union Pacific Railroad's official photographer, Andrew J. Russell, captured this iconic photograph of the Central Pacific's engine *Jupiter* nearly touching cowcatchers with the Union Pacific's engine *No. 119* at Promontory Point, Utah, on May 10, 1869. Railroad promoters upset by the display of drinking evident in this picture released a "clean" copy without the presence of bottles.

– TRUE WEST ARCHIVES –

the picturesque valley. Today, visitors can stay in the lodge, tour the museum in the original trading post, and enjoy the spectacular views of Monument Valley known worldwide.

1000 Main St
Monument Valley, UT 84536
435-727-3231 • Gouldings.com

Moab

The earliest Mormon settlers of Moab in the 1850s were driven out by Indian attacks. In 1878, a new wave of settlers restarted the community. The isolated, rural river town attracted its share of miscreants, including Harvey Alexander Logan, aka Kid Curry, who on May 26, 1900, went on a killing spree of revenge in Moab, killing Grand County Sheriff Jesse Tyler and Deputy Sam Jenkins. Tyler had killed his friend George "Flatnose" Curry (Logan's adopted last name) and his brother, Larry Logan. Visitors should start their tour at the Museum of Moab before venturing out to drive three scenic byways and visit Canyonlands and Arches National Parks and Dead Horse Point State Park.

217 Center St, Moab, UT 84532
435-259-5121 • DiscoverMoab.com

Meadow Mountains Massacre Site

The site commemorates an attack on an Arkansas emigrant wagon train by Mormon settlers with local Paiute Indians. The local Latter-day Saints pioneers were suspicious of the federal government's anti-Mormon policies, and on September 11, 1857, the Mormon militia attacked and killed 120 men, women and children of the Baker-Fancher wagon train. Seventeen children survived. The National Historic Landmark is 40 minutes north of present-day St. George on State Highway 18.

MountainMeadowsMassacre.com
MTN-Meadows-Assoc.com

Monument Valley

Monument Valley became known internationally after Harry and Leone "Mike" Goulding convinced John Ford to make his movie *Stagecoach* amidst the valley's beautiful buttes in 1938. Today, nearly 80 years later, Monument Valley is one of the most iconic sites in the American West. Visitors can stay at the Navajo Nation's recently built View Lodge, in which every room has a balcony view of the sunrise over Monument Valley Navajo Tribal Park. Tourists can take a 3.2-mile self-guided walking tour, a 17-mile scenic loop drive or hire a Navajo guide for a personal tour through the park.

Navajo Nation Reservation accessible from U.S. Highway 163. • 928-871-6647
NavajoNationParks.org

Robbers Roost

Butch Cassidy's gang found refuge in Utah Territory's rugged Capitol Reef Country. North of Hanksville, visitors drive north on State Highway 24 and follow the Robber's Roost Trail, a 28-mile dirt road for ATV and ORV and four-wheel-drive vehicles only. From the parking area, trails lead into historic sites in the back country, including Butch Cassidy's cabin and camping area.

Hanksville, UT • 800-858-7951
NPS.gov / CapitolReef.org

This is the Place Heritage Park

A living history village dedicated to the Mormon settlement in Utah, This is the Place Heritage Park commemorates where Brigham Young and his Church of Latter-day Saints pioneers viewed the Salt Lake Valley from the foothills of the Wasatch Mountains at the mouth of Emigrant Canyon. Young declared "this is the place," and today the location

is an interactive history center, where visitors can tour a Pioneer Village of restored and replicated 19th-century homes, buildings and businesses, an Indian Village and ride around the park on two miniature trains.

2601 Sunnyside Ave
Salt Lake City, UT 84108 • 801-582-1847
ThisIsThePlace.org

Wyoming
Buffalo

Visitors who walk the downtown district of Buffalo, Wyoming, should consider spending the night and dining at the Occidental Hotel, where Owen Wister may have written part of his famous novel, *The Virginian.* The Jim Gatchell Memorial Museum's exhibits chronicle local history, including the Johnson County War. Just outside town is the TA Ranch, a historic guest ranch that was the site of a major conflict during the cattle war. Don't miss Longmire Days every July in celebration of writer Craig Johnson's Walt Longmire mystery novels and television series set in Big Horn Country.

55 N. Main St, Buffalo, WY 82834
800-227-5122 • *BuffaloWyoming.org*

Cody

Cody, Wyoming, is one of the preeminent Western destinations. Founded as a land venture to attract the railroad near the

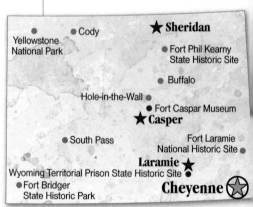

The Last Supper of Outlaw Photos. The "Fort Worth Five" is how this iconic 1900 photograph of a quintet of Wild Bunch members (left to right, Sundance Kid, Will Carver, Ben Kilpatrick, Harvey Logan and Butch Cassidy) is known today. "The Curse of the Fort Worth Five" would be a more accurate title. All five men died violent deaths. Will Carver was shot to death by Texas police in 1901. A wounded, cornered Harvey Logan committed suicide in a Colorado field in 1904. High in the Andes, a wounded, cornered Butch Cassidy shot a wounded, cornered Sundance, then shot himself. Ben Kilpatrick survived the longest, only because he spent ten years in prison, out of harm's way. He died at the hands of an ice-mallet wielding express messenger during a botched Texas train robbery in 1912.

– PHOTO FROM THE PINKERTON DETECTIVE AGENCY, TRUE WEST ARCHIVES –

east entrance of Yellowstone, William F. "Buffalo Bill" Cody lent his name to the town. Begin your tour by checking into Cody's Historic Irma Hotel (don't miss the cherry wood bar given to Cody by Queen Victoria), named after his daughter, and then visiting the Buffalo Bill Center of the West's complex of five museums, library and archive, the most significant Western history museum center in the United States. Schedule a couple of days to tour the Buffalo Bill History Museum, Cody Firearms Museum, Plains Indian Museum, Draper Museum of Natural History and the Whitney Gallery of Western Art.

836 Sheridan Ave, Cody, WY 82414
307-587-2297 • CodyChamber.com

Fort Bridger State Historic Site

In 1843, mountain men Jim Bridger and Louis Vasquez opened a trading post along the Oregon Trail. In the early 1850s, it became a Mormon outpost and then an Army camp in 1858. Visitors can walk along the Oregon Trail at the site, tour restored and reconstructed historical buildings and the museum in the 1888 stone barracks. Every Labor Day Weekend, the annual Fort Bridger Rendezvous brings the park alive with an encampment of re-enactors.

37000 I-80 Business Loop
Fort Bridger, WY 82933
307-782-3842 • WyoParks.State.WY.us

Fort Phil Kearny State Historic Site, located near Banner, between Buffalo and Sheridan, Wyoming, is dedicated to interpreting the history of the Bozeman Trail, the U.S. incursion onto Sioux lands and the subsequent Red Cloud War.

– COURTESY WYOMING OFFICE OF TOURISM –

Fort Laramie National Historic Site

Established in 1834 to serve the transcontinental fur trade, Fort Laramie's location on the North Platte River and the overland trail assured its role as a military fort, trading post and key stopping point for hundreds of thousands of emigrants traveling to the West. A strategic post during the Plains Indian Wars, Fort Laramie also was a station stop for the Pony Express and Overland Stage. Visitors to the who take the self-guided or guided tour will learn the importance of Fort Laramie to U.S. history until its closure in 1890.

965 Gray Rocks Rd
Fort Laramie, WY 82212
307-837-2221 • NPS.gov

Fort Caspar Museum

Originally built in 1865 as Platte Bridge Station, the city of Casper manages the reconstructed fort as a living history museum. Adjacent to the North Platte River and the national emigrant trails, Fort Caspar was an Army camp for just two years before the post was closed and the troops transferred to Fort Fetterman. Rebuilt by the WPA in the 1930s, visitors to the fort should tour the museum and the fort's well-furnished complex of historic army facilities and barracks.

200 N David, Casper, WY 82601
307-234-3260
FortCasparWyoming.com

Fort Phil Kearny State Historic Site

In the foothills of the Big Horn Mountains, the Fort Phil Kearny State Historic Site commemorates the ill-fated 1866 fort built on the Bozeman Trail during the Red Cloud War. The fort was burned after the Army abandoned it in 1868. Today, visitors can tour a replica of the fort and take a walking tour of interpretive sites about Red Cloud's Indian who wiped out Capt. William Fetterman's entire command of 80 soldiers.

528 Wagon Box Rd, Banner, WY 82832
307-684-7629 • FortPhilKearny.com

Hole-in-the-Wall

Forty miles southwest from Kaycee in the Big Horn Mountains, the legendary Hole-in-the-Wall outlaw hideaway is managed by the BLM. Outlaws Butch Cassidy and his Wild Bunch Gang were known to ride through the "hole" in the sandstone wall to escape from the law. The site is accessible only by primitive roads and a 2.5-mile cross-country hike. Always check with the field office for current conditions, a map and directions.

Interstate 25 south from Kaycee to the TTT Road exit. At TTT Road exit, drive south about 14 miles to Willow Creek Road (County Road 111). Take this road west for about 18 miles to a primitive two-track road which bears north. This is County Road 105, which has a number of livestock gates. • BLM.gov

Sheridan

In 1882 John D. Loucks founded Sheridan, which he named in honor of his commanding officer in the Civil War. The gateway city to the Big Horn Mountains and Little Big Horn country of Montana, Sheridan became an economic center for the bi-state region after the railroad arrived in 1892. Today, visitors can stay at the fully restored Sheridan Inn, stroll historic downtown and tour the Brinton, Sheridan County and Bozeman Trail museums.

1517 E 5th St Sheridan, WY 82801
307-673-7121
SheridanWyoming.org

South Pass City

South Pass City is one of the best preserved mining towns in the state. Gold Rush Days are held every July in the boomtown adjacent to the famous pass through the Rocky Mountains. The town is open to tour, with a small admission fee, May 14 through September 30. Prior to the 1867 gold rush, South Pass was best known as the key crossing point of the

Continental Divide for emigrants and travelers on the Overland Trail.

Fremont County, WY. T27N/R102W. The Buttes are visible from the BLM interpretive overlook for South Pass located about 47 miles southwest of Lander on State Route 28. SouthPassCity.com

Yellowstone National Park

The nation's—and world's—first national park, Yellowstone National Park was created on March 1, 1872, when President Ulysses S. Grant signed it into law. Yellowstone is also one of the largest national parks, at 2,291,791 acres. The first rangers to patrol the

This studio portrait of the Sundance Kid and Etta Place was made by DeYoung's in New York, 1901. Robert Leroy Parker (inset), alias Butch Cassidy, is shown here in an 1894 mug shot taken during his tenure at Wyoming Territorial Prison in Laramie.

– SUNDANCE & ETTA COURTESY LIBRARY OF CONGRESS, PINKERTON COLLECTION; BUTCH CASSIDY, TRUE WEST ARCHIVES –

The surveyors of the West went to great lengths to accomplish their enormous tasks, using whatever transportation was needed. In 1871, William Henry Jackson photographed members of the Hayden Survey on *Annie*, the first boat on Yellowstone Lake.

– COURTESY YELLOWSTONE NATIONAL PARK –

park were members of a U.S. Cavalry troop, which in 1877 was called out to protect tourists from Chief Joseph's Nez Perce warriors. Visit the Albright Visitor Center to learn about the role of the U.S. Cavalry at Yellowstone.

PO Box 168
Yellowstone National Park, WY 82190
307-344-7381• *NPS.gov*

Wyoming Territorial Prison State Historic Site

Built in 1872, the Wyoming Territorial Prison held the West's most violent and desperate outlaws (including the notorious Butch Cassidy) during the dramatic time of Wyoming's federal Territorial days and early statehood. The Wyoming Prison is now a museum, and includes a new exhibit on Butch Cassidy. Visitors can tour the warden's quarters, the horse barn, prison industries broom factory, visitor center, historic buildings, as well as picnic and enjoy a nature trail.

975 Snowy Range Rd
Laramie, WY 82070 • 307-745-3733
WyomingTerritorialPrison.com

Great Books

American Carnage: Wounded Knee, 1890 *by Jerome A Greene* (University of Oklahoma Press, 2014)

Black Kettle : The Cheyenne Chief Who Sought Peace but Found War *by Thom Hatch* (Wiley, 2004)

Charles M. Russell: Photographing the Legend *by Larry Len Peterson* (University of Oklahoma Press, 2014)

Crazy Horse: The Strange Man of the Oglalas 3rd Edition, *by Mari Sandoz, Introduction by Vine Deloria Jr.* (Bison Books, 2008)

Custer's Trials: A Life on the Frontier of a New America *by T.J. Stiles* (Knopf, 2015)

Give Your Heart to the Hawks: A Tribute to the Mountain Men *by Win Blevins* (Nash Publishing, 1973)

Jim Bridger *by Stanley Vestal* (University of Nebraska Press, 1970)

Mountain Man: John Colter, the Lewis & Clark Expedition, and the Call of the American West *by David Weston Marshall* (The Countryman Press, 2017)

Nothing Like It in the World: The Men Who Built the Transcontinental Railroad, 1863-1869 *by Stephen E. Ambrose* (Simon & Schuster, 2000)

Ride the Wind *by Lucia St. Clair Robson* (Ballantine, 1982)

Rocky Mountain Mining Camps *by Duane A. Smith* (University of Indiana Press, 1967)

The Bloody Bozeman: The Perilous Trail to Montana's Gold *by Dorothy M. Johnson* (McGraw Hill, 1971)

The Journey of Crazy Horse: A Lakota History *by Joseph M. Marshall* (Viking, 2004)

The Last Outlaws: The Lives and Legends of Butch Cassidy and the Sundance Kid *by Thom Hatch* (NAL, 2013)

Tom Horn: In Life and Legend *by Larry D. Ball* (University of Oklahoma Press, 2014)

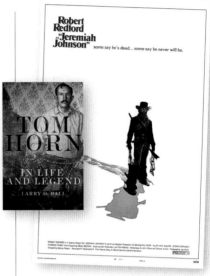

— COURTESY WARNER BROS. —

Western Film & TV

Butch Cassidy and the Sundance Kid (*20th Century Fox, 1969*)

Centennial (*NBC, 1978*)

Dances With Wolves (*Orion, 1990*)

Heaven's Gate (*United Artists, 1980*)

Jeremiah Johnson (*Warner Bros., 1971*)

Monte Walsh (*National General Pictures, 1970*)

Pale Rider (*Warner Bros., 1980*)

Shane (*Paramount, 1953*)

The Cowboys (*Warner Bros., 1972*)

The Missouri Breaks (*United Artists, 1976*)

The Mountain Men (*Columbia, 1980*)

The Mystic Warrior (*ABC, 1984*)

Tom Horn (*Warner Bros., 1980*)

Union Pacific (*Paramount, 1939*)

Beyond Custer Hill

June 25, 1876

Lieutenant Colonel George Armstrong Custer's mind is racing with military strategies and tactics. As usual, he is reacting to a fluid battle situation (something at which he's a genius).

After ordering Maj. Marcus Reno to attack a large Indian village nestled in Montana's Little Bighorn Valley, Custer notices 50 "hostiles" on his right flank and gives chase. When they scatter, Custer keeps going, leading his command north. As he rides, he formulates a new battle plan without telling his other commanders (this is one of Custer's biggest faults as a leader).

Now he's looking for a river crossing as his battalion continues north at a gallop along the barren shoulders of the Little Bighorn River (see map, opposite page).

The regiment turns into a broad, fantail ravine and follows it down. As they traverse the gully, Custer's command starts taking fire from the rear. Wolf Tooth, a Cheyenne who had been scouting with 40 to 50 warriors, sees the soldiers heading for the village and opens fire.

With Indians behind him, Custer cannot commit his entire command, so he sends Algernon Smith and E Troop to test the crossing. Meanwhile, Custer and four companies hang back, riding the ridgeline above the river as a rear guard.

On Smith's return, Custer learns that the ford at Dry Creek (a.k.a. Muskrat Creek) is "too miry" and full of bogs.

A small number of warriors (believed to be four) are defending this crossing from the village side, but more important, Smith notes that the Indians,

Custer: Everything that can go wrong, does.

– ILLUSTRATIONS BY BOB BOZE BELL –

mostly noncombatants, are fleeing to the west and northwest. This is Custer's worst fear: that the inhabitants of the camp will escape.

Now Custer is even more determined to find a crossing that will head off the fleeing Indians.

Wolf Tooth and his warriors continue harassing and sniping at the troops from long range, but Custer is not yet worried. He has been in hundreds of fights during his storied Civil War career and is considered by some to be the top Indian fighter in the U.S. Army.

Custer leaves three of his five companies—I, C and L—fighting Wolf Tooth's men (and to act as a connection when Capt. Frederick Benteen and the pack train come up). With Companies E and F, Custer rides northwest off the ridgeline and into a broad plain that empties toward the river. As Custer and his troops approach the river bank, they are fired on by a group of warriors who are guarding the women and children.

Superior firepower keeps the Indians at bay for the first hour of the fight. Wolf Tooth and his warriors stay way back in the tall grass, away from the long range of the soldier's Springfields. (The .45-70 caliber trapdoor carbines can accurately fire 300 yards beyond a Winchester.) As more and more warriors spill onto the battlefield from the Reno sector, however, the Custer skirmishers are overwhelmed as increasing numbers of Indians stalk them in the tall grass. The Indians have at least 200 repeating rifles (according to archaeologists).

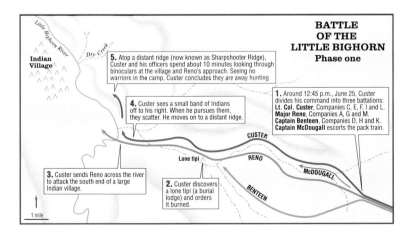

BATTLE OF THE LITTLE BIGHORN
Phase one

Indian Village

Little Bighorn River   Dry Creek

5. Atop a distant ridge (now known as Sharpshooter Ridge), Custer and his officers spend about 10 minutes looking through binoculars at the village and Reno's approach. Seeing no warriors in the camp, Custer concludes they are away hunting

4. Custer sees a small band of Indians off to his right. When he pursues them, they scatter. He moves on to a distant ridge.

1. Around 12:45 p.m., June 25, Custer divides his command into three battalions: Lt. Col. Custer, Companies C, E, F, I and L. Major Reno, Companies A, G and M. Captain Benteen, Companies D, H and K. Captain McDougall escorts the pack train.

CUSTER

Lone tipi   RENO

3. Custer sends Reno across the river to attack the south end of a large Indian village.

2. Custer discovers a lone tipi (a burial lodge) and orders it burned.

McDOUGALL

BENTEEN

1 mile

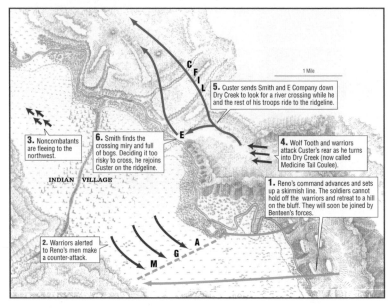

5. Custer sends Smith and E Company down Dry Creek to look for a river crossing while he and the rest of his troops ride to the ridgeline.

3. Noncombatants are fleeing to the northwest.

6. Smith finds the crossing miry and full of bogs. Deciding it too risky to cross, he rejoins Custer on the ridgeline.

4. Wolf Tooth and warriors attack Custer's rear as he turns into Dry Creek (now called Medicine Tail Coulee).

1. Reno's command advances and sets up a skirmish line. The soldiers cannot hold off the warriors and retreat to a hill on the bluff. They will soon be joined by Benteen's forces.

INDIAN VILLAGE

2. Warriors alerted to Reno's men make a counter-attack.

1 Mile

Members of F Company dismount and form a skirmish line. Instead of having his troopers each hold three horses (see 1876 cavalry tactics, p. 121), Custer orders more firepower on the ground and has them each hold eight horses (a bold but risky technique he used on the Yellowstone three years earlier). Indians waving blankets and shooting cause the soldiers' horses to stampede. Warriors quickly capture them. With most of F Troop on foot, Custer knows the entire operation and his command are in grave peril.

While Custer attempts this second crossing, word is sent to the warriors fighting Reno that soldiers are trying to capture the women and children. Virtually all the Indian combatants in the Reno sector disengage and race pell-mell toward the slopes above the north end of the village.

Meanwhile, F Company is retreating back toward the ridgeline, where the rest of the command has gathered, as Company E (which still has its horses) lays down covering fire. After a one-mile run, F Company finally gains the top of a ridge. E Company dismounts and fights

Dismounted troopers establish a skirmish line as the "led horses" are taken over the hill for safekeeping. This backfires when Chief Gall and other warriors sneak up on them and stampede the horses.

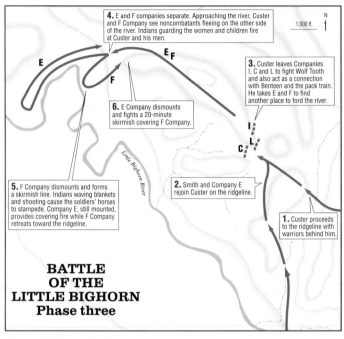

4. E and F companies separate. Approaching the river, Custer and F Company see noncombatants fleeing on the other side of the river. Indians guarding the women and children fire at Custer and his men.

1,000 ft.   N

3. Custer leaves Companies I, C and L to fight Wolf Tooth and also act as a connection with Benteen and the pack train. He takes E and F to find another place to ford the river.

6. E Company dismounts and fights a 20-minute skirmish covering F Company.

5. F Company dismounts and forms a skirmish line. Indians waving blankets and shooting cause the soldiers' horses to stampede. Company E, still mounted, provides covering fire while F Company retreats toward the ridgeline.

2. Smith and Company E rejoin Custer on the ridgeline.

1. Custer proceeds to the ridgeline with warriors behind him.

Little Bighorn River

BATTLE OF THE LITTLE BIGHORN
Phase three

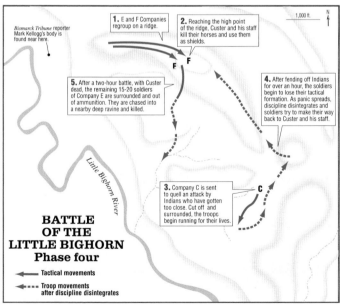

1. E and F Companies regroup on a ridge.

2. Reaching the high point of the ridge, Custer and his staff kill their horses and use them as shields.

1,000 ft.   N

Bismarck Tribune reporter Mark Kellogg's body is found near here.

5. After a two-hour battle, with Custer dead, the remaining 15-20 soldiers of Company E are surrounded and out of ammunition. They are chased into a nearby deep ravine and killed.

4. After fending off Indians for over an hour, the soldiers begin to lose their tactical formation. As panic spreads, discipline disintegrates and soldiers try to make their way back to Custer and his staff.

3. Company C is sent to quell an attack by Indians who have gotten too close. Cut off and surrounded, the troops begin running for their lives.

Little Bighorn River

BATTLE OF THE LITTLE BIGHORN
Phase four

→ Tactical movements

◀---- Troop movements after discipline disintegrates

Battle: By Bob Boze Bell

England-born, Minnesota-raised photographer William H. Illingworth had earned a strong reputation as a photographer on army expeditions on the Northern Plains when he was hired in 1874 to accompany the famous Custer Expedition into the Black Hills.

– TRUE WEST ARCHIVES –

In 1879, Capt. George Sanderson and his 11th Infantry were sent out to the battlefield to clean it up. Photographer Stanley Morrow accompanied them, and he captured this grisly scene of bones and equipment, still strewn across the hills and gullies. In the foreground are a soldier's boot soles. The Indians had no use for the soles and would cut off the bottoms and keep the tops for pouches or other uses. There is only one known earlier photo taken of Last Stand Hill in 1877 by Fouch. In this photo, the horses' skulls still have hair. The photo is in a private collection.

– TRUE WEST ARCHIVES –

in a skirmish line to cover its horseless comrades. A 20-minute gunfight ensues while Custer desperately tries to stall until the pack train and reinforcements arrive. (Custer's brother Boston has told him both are six miles away.)

As the Indians become increasingly bolder, more and more cavalry horses are stampeded and captured. A charge by C Company to drive back some of the newly arriving Indians meets with disaster as the soldiers are cut off and surrounded. Half of Company C's soldiers die, and panic sets in all along the skirmish line as troopers bunch together and begin to run.

With over half of his command unhorsed, Custer realizes his only hope is for Capt. Benteen and Maj. Reno to save him.

Helplessly watching the collapse of his command, Custer and his headquarters staff kill horses to make breastworks on the highest point of a hillock. Panicked soldiers begin running toward the hill as Indian suicide riders step up their bold attacks.

As if things could not get any worse for Custer, most of the warriors (an estimated 1,500) who were fighting Reno now come pouring onto the battlefield from the south, across the bluffs, through the water and up all the draws and coulees.

Company E holds a position west and below Custer's location to protect Custer's flank from warriors who are moving in from the northwest. In spite of this, suicide warriors successfully get past Company E and stampede all of the troopers' remaining horses.

A two-hour gun battle that started slowly now gains a frightening momentum as waves of warriors on horseback and on foot quickly overrun the few able soldiers on the hilltop with Custer and kill them all.

With some 190 dead and dying soldiers strewn for hundreds of yards, the warriors turn their attention to the 15-20 men from Company E, who are surrounded, on foot and out of ammunition. Gamely, these men make a run for it, many still carrying their empty weapons to use as clubs. They are all chased into a deep ravine and killed. The battle is over.

The controversy begins.

Custer had two horses with him on the campaign: Vic (Victory) and Dandy. In battle, he rode Vic (at right), who had a white blaze on his face and three white stockings. Historian Michael Donahue believes the Indians took Vic with them to Canada. In contrast, one field report stated that Vic was found dead, 100-150 feet from Custer, and another stated Vic was one of the dead horses making up the breastworks near where Custer died. Dandy (at left) was with the pack train and not only survived, but was also sent back to the Custer family.

Hayden Survey photographer William Henry Jackson's landscapes of the Yellowstone country, including an encampment by a small lake between East Fork and Yellowstone Lake, helped influence President Ulysses S. Grant to create Yellowstone National Park.

– COURTESY YELLOWSTONE NATIONAL PARK –

Northern Prairie and Plains

Iowa, Minnesota, North Dakota and South Dakota

The Northern Prairies and Plains of the West are awe-inspiring in their natural beauty, endless vistas, rolling hills, dense forests and long, winding river valleys. Today, millions of acres of land are planted with grains that feed a world, where tens of millions of bison once roamed and nomadic Indian tribes followed with the seasons. From the legendary shores of Minnesota's Lake Superior to the mystical Black Hills of South Dakota, from the banks of the Mississippi where William F. Cody was born in the Iowa Territory to the historic earthen lodge Indian villages of North Dakota, visitors to the Northern Prairie and Plains will discover a region rich in history, culture and heritage.

Mount Rushmore, South Dakota

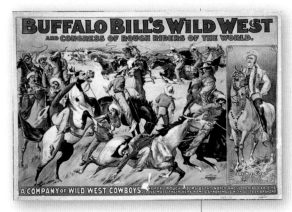

Buffalo Bill's Wild West entertained audiences across the United States and around the world from 1883 to 1913.

– LIBRARY OF CONGRESS –

Iowa

Buffalo Bill Museum

The Mississippi River town of LeClaire has a rich Western heritage, including being the birthplace of William F. "Buffalo Bill" Cody on February 26, 1846. The Buffalo Bill Museum has a broad collection that celebrates the region's history, and the LeClaire's Famous Sons exhibit. After visiting LeClaire, take a short drive to tour the Buffalo Bill Cody Homestead in Scott County.

200 N Cody Rd, Le Claire, IA 52753
563-289-5580
BuffaloBillMuseumLeClaire.com
ScottCountyIowa.Com

The Fort Museum & Frontier Village

In May 1850, a U.S. soldiers were sent from Minnesota to build a fort on the Des Moines River in Iowa. Fort Dodge was named in honor of Wisconsin Senator Col. Henry Dodge, who in 1833 had founded the 1st U.S. Dragoons. The fort was sold to the post sutler William Williams in 1853, who then platted out the town of Fort Dodge. The Fort Museum & Frontier Village is an interactive history center that honors the town's role in the settlement of Iowa.

614 9th St, Fort Madison, IA 52627
515-573-4231 • *FortMuseum.com*

John Wayne Birthplace & Museum

On May 27, 1907, Marion Robert Morrison was born in Winterset, the son of Clyde and Mary Brown Morrison. The Iowan from Madison County would grow up to be film star John Wayne. Today, the John Wayne Birthplace & Museum is a destination for the iconic Westerner's fans worldwide. Tour the museum just off Winterset's historic town square which was dedicated in 2015, his humble

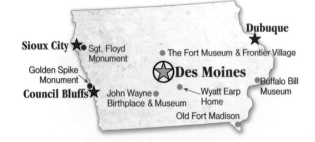

The John Wayne Birthplace and Museum in Winterset, Iowa, which includes John Wayne's childhood home, is the world's only museum dedicated to the life and career of the iconic Western film star.

– STUART ROSEBROOK –

childhood home, and plan on attending the museum's biggest annual event—the two-day John Wayne Birthday Celebration held every May.

205 John Wayne Dr, Winterset, IA 50273
877-462-1044
JohnWayneBirthplace.museum

Golden Spike Monument
In 1862 Congress determined that the Union Pacific Railroad Company would start construction on the eastern shore of the Missouri River in Council Bluffs. In 1939, as a promotion for the film *Union Pacific*, the 56-foot Golden Spike Monument was dedicated in Council Bluffs at Mile Marker Zero of the rail line. When in Council Bluffs, don't miss the Historic General Dodge House, the Lincoln Monument, the Union Pacific Railroad Museum and the Western Historic Trails Center.

2073-2099 9th Ave
Council Bluffs, IA 51501
712-256-257 • *TravelCouncilBluffs.com*

Old Fort Madison
Fort Madison was built along the Mississippi River in 1808, 38 years before Iowa was a state. An outpost until 1813, it is the oldest American fort on the Upper Mississippi, and was attacked by the British during the War of 1812. Old Fort Madison provides an extraordinary historical interpretation of the earliest decades of American trans-Appalachian history, including annual re-enactment events.

614 9th St, Fort Madison, IA 52627
319-372-6318 • *FortMadison.com*

Wyatt Earp, in his early 20s in 1869 or 1870, a few years before his legendary life as a Western lawman began in Wichita, Kansas, in 1874. Before his career as a lawman, his family moved back and forth from Illinois to Iowa. His childhood home in Pella, Iowa, is preserved as the Wyatt Earp Home-Van Spanckeren House in the Pella Historical Museum Village.

– COURTESY JEFF MOREY –

Sergeant Floyd Monument

Sgt. Charles Floyd was the only member of the Corps of Discovery to die on the Lewis and Clark expedition. He died of appendicitis on August 20, 1804, and was buried on a bluff near the river. The Sergeant Floyd Monument, a 100-foot Egyptian-style obelisk above the Missouri River, was dedicated in his honor in 1901.

2601 S Lewis Blvd, Sioux City, IA 51103
800-593-222
VisitSiouxCity.org / NPS.gov

Wyatt Earp Home

The Wyatt Earp Home-Van Spanckeren House is home to the Pella Historical Museum Village, dedicated to the history of the 800 Dutch settlers who founded Pella in 1846. The house's first-floor apartment was also the childhood home of Wyatt Earp in the early 1860s. Visitors to the museum will learn what life was like for the Earps, who twice lived in Pella between 1849 and 1864.

507 Franklin St, Pella, IA 50219
641-628-2409
PellaHistoricalMuseum.wordpress.com

Minnesota
Fort Ridgely State Park

Built in 1855 adjacent to the Dakota Sioux Reservation in the Minnesota River Valley, Fort Ridgely played a key role in the U.S.-Dakota War of 1862. Ten years after the war the fort was shuttered and sold. In 1896 a war memorial was built on the site, and in 1911 the state bought the property for a park. Start at the visitors center and tour the interpretive exhibit, which requires a small entrance fee.

72158 County Rd 30, Fairfax, MN 55332
507-426-7840 • *DNR.State.MN.us*

Grand Portage National Monument

Grand Portage National Monument is co-managed with the Minnesota Chippewa Tribe-Grand Portage Band, and is the most important national park living history center dedicated to the Old Northwest Euro-American fur trade network. Tours should begin at the visitors center and proceed to the re-created fort on the shore of Lake Superior. Grand Portage's signature annual event is the Rendezvous Days and Powwow staged the second week of every August.

Grand Portage, MN 55605
218-475-0123 • *NPS.gov*

James J. Hill House

The James J. Hill House in St. Paul was the largest and most expensive ever built in Minnesota when it was completed in 1891. The Gilded Age mansion remained the railroad baron's family home until 1925 when his heirs donated it to the Catholic Diocese. The Minnesota Historical Society has owned and managed it as a museum since 1978 and it's now a National Historic Landmark.

240 Summit Ave, St. Paul, MN 55102
651-297-2555 • Sites.MNSH.org

Historic Fort Snelling

Historic Fort Snelling brings history to life at the Army outpost first built in 1825. Located at the confluence of the Minnesota and Mississippi rivers, the U.S. built the outpost to keep the peace in the rich fur trading region of the Upper Mississippi River Valley. Visitors today enjoy touring the exhibits, attending special history programs and walking the grounds of the fort that served the Army until 1946.

200 Tower Ave, St Paul, MN 55111
612-726-1171 • HistoricFortSnelling.org

Madelia

Following the failed robbery of the First National Bank in Northfield on September 7, 1876, the James-Younger Gang fled southwest and then split up in an attempt to escape being brought to justice. Two weeks and a 100 miles later, on September 21, 1876, Charlie Pitts and Cole, Jim and Bob Younger were cornered in Hanska Slough outside of Madelia. Each year during the third week of September, the town of Madelia holds a re-enactment of the Younger Brothers' Capture that celebrates the townspeople's role in the enthralling saga of the failed Northfield Bank Robbery.

127 W Main St, Madelia, MN 50602
507-642-8822 • MadeliaMN.com

North West Company Fur Post

Near Pine City, the Minnesota Historical Society's North West Company Fur Post brings history alive at the reconstructed 1804 trading center. A museum dedicated to the French voyageur and British fur trade era presents extraordinary exhibits while rangers dressed in period costume conduct educational history programs. A heritage trail on the Snake River is open throughout the year for recreation.

12551 Voyageur Ln, Pine City, MN 55063
320-629-6356 • Sites.MNHS.org

Northfield Historic District

Founded in 1855, Northfield entered the history books permanently as the legendary site of the James-Younger Gang's failed robbery of the First National Bank on September 7, 1876. Visitors to Northfield should tour the historic downtown after touring Northfield's Historical Society and Museum, in the restored original bank building. The annual Defeat of Jesse James Days is held every Labor Day

Grand Portage National Monument ●

Duluth ★

North West Company Fur Post ●

Minneapolis ★

James J. Hill House ● ⊛ St. Paul
Historic Fort Snelling ●

Northfield Historic District ●
New Ulm ★

● Fort Ridgely State Park
● Pipestone ● Madelia
National Monument

Weekend and is one of the premiere Old West re-enactment events in the region.

Northfield Area Chamber of Commerce
205 Third St West, Suite B, Northfield, MN 55057 507-645-5604
VisitingNorthfield.com
NorthfieldHistory.org

Pipestone National Monument

For 3,000 years, the American Indian stone quarry at Pipestone National Monument has been actively used for making pipes. A monument since 1937, the quarry was saved by the Yankton Sioux tribe of South Dakota and can be used by members of federally recognized American Indian tribes. Tour the visitors center, watch Native pipestone carving demonstrations and walk the Circle Trail to see the most important features of the park.

36 Reservation Ave, Pipestone, MN 56164
507-825-5464 • *NPS.gov*

North Dakota

Camp Hancock State Historic Site

Visitors to North Dakota's state capital, Bismarck, should visit Camp Hancock State Historic Site, dedicated to interpreting local history at the military encampment built to protect the construction crews of the Northern Pacific Railroad in 1872.

101 E Main Ave, Bismarck, ND 58501
701-328-2666 • *History.ND.gov*

Fort Ambercrombie State Historic Site

Nicknamed "the Gateway to the Dakotas," Fort Ambercrombie was the first American fort built in the Dakota Territory in 1858. During the U.S.-Dakota War of 1862, the post was under siege for six weeks. Abandoned in 1877, the fort was reconstructed in the 1930s to be an interactive history center, with programs held throughout the year, with most taking place during the summer months.

935 Broadway, Abercrombie, ND 58001
701-553-8513• *History.ND.gov*

Fort Buford State Historic Site

Near the confluence of the Yellowstone and Missouri rivers, Fort Buford was constructed in 1866 as a key Army supply depot to support the Northern Plains campaigns. In service for 29 years, Fort Buford is best known as the 1881 surrender site of Sitting Bull. Across the Missouri River from Fort Union Trading Post National Historic Site, Fort Buford offers visitors an opportunity to walk into the past of frontier North Dakota.

15349 39th Ln NW, Williston, ND 58801
701-572-9034 • *History.ND.gov*

Fort Totten State Historic Site

On the banks of Devils Lake, Fort Totten State Historic Site stands as a testament to frontier, military and Indian life in the Dakota Territory after the Civil

Fort Union Trading Post National Historic Site
Fort Buford State Historic Site
★ Williston
Gingras Trading Post State Historic Site •
Fort Totten State Historic Site
Fargo ★
● Killdeer Mountain Battlefield State Historic Site
Medora
★ Dickinson
● Camp Hancock State Historic Site
Theodore Roosevelt National Park
★ Bismarck
Knife River Indian Villages National Historic Site
Fort Ambercrombie State Historic Site

The Fort Union Trading Post National Historic Site near Williston, North Dakota, hosts three major events annually: Fort Union Rendezvous in mid-June, Indian Arts Showcase in early August and Living History Weekend every Labor Day weekend.

War. Built in 1868-'73 as a key outpost adjacent to the Devils Lake Sioux Reservation, the fort was converted to an Indian school in 1890. Visitors can tour many of the original buildings, including the commissary storehouse, which houses the Fort Totten Interpretive Center.

SE edge of Fort Totten, ND, 13 miles SE of Devils Lake • 701-328-2666 • History.ND.gov

Fort Union Trading Post National Historic Site

A major living history center along the Lewis and Clark National Historic Trail, Fort Union Trading Post was built in 1826 at the confluence of the Missouri and Yellowstone rivers. An international trading center, Fort Union was a crossroads of history for four decades, serving most of the famed mountain men and Indian tribes of the era. Every summer the park hosts events with re-enactors in period dress, including the Fort Union Rendezvous.

15550 Hwy 1804, Williston, ND 58801 701-572-9083 • NPS.gov

Gingras Trading Post State Historic Site

Near Walhalla in northeastern North Dakota near the Manitoba border, Gingras Trading Post State Historic Site interprets and preserves Antoine Blanc Gingras's 1840s trading post and home. A Métis fur trader, his restored two-story post and separate home are rare examples of early settlements in the state. Visitors will enjoy the museum in the finely appointed home, and souvenirs of the fur trade can be purchased in the Gingras store.

12882 129th Ave NE, Walhalla, ND 58282 701-549-2775 • History.ND.gov

Knife River Indian Villages National Historic Site

For 500 years, the Knife River Indian Villages were the traditional home of the Hidatsa people, and later the Mandan and Arikira. They were a major Native tribal trading center on the Missouri River for centuries before the arrival of Europeans. In the 1750s a fur trading center was established. Tour the visitors center to learn about the role of the

The Battle of Northfield

September 7, 1876

It's just past 2 p.m. when three horsemen wearing matching white linen dusters dismount in front of the First National Bank in Northfield, Minnesota. After tying their reins to hitching posts, they stroll to the corner (see Phase One, p. 61), sit on some dry goods boxes and exchange pleasantries with several locals.

Two more horsemen, also wearing linen dusters, approach up Division Street from the south. Several minutes later, three more horsemen, dressed in matching dusters, cross the iron bridge and stop in the center of Mill Square. The three men seated on the corner stand up, walk back to the bank and then go inside.

Two mounted men, who came from the south, pull up in front of the bank. One of them, Cole Younger, says under his breath, "You'd better close the door," and they both dismount. His partner, Clell Miller, leads his horse to the bank door and shuts it. In the middle of the street, Cole scans the roadway while pretending to tighten the cinch on his saddle.

Several townsmen are suspicious of all the uniformed strangers, and one local, J.S. Allen, walks to the bank and looks in the window. His suspicions

confirmed, Allen turns to go alert the other citizens when he is confronted by Miller, who has just closed the door. Grabbing Allen by the collar, the outlaw says, "You son of a bitch, don't you holler." Allen breaks free and runs up the boardwalk, shouting, "Get your guns boys. They're robbing the bank!"

Cole immediately mounts and pulls his revolver, firing it in the air as a signal for the three horsemen in Mill Square to come quick—they have been discovered.

At almost the same instant, those outside hear a shot from inside the bank. The three horsemen from the square pull their pistols and ride into the engagement, firing and yelling at bystanders to "get in."

Miller grabs the reins of his horse to mount up. As he steps into the stirrup, birdshot pellets fired by local Elias Stacy hit Miller in the face, and he falls backward to the ground. Another townsman, A.R. Manning, aims his single-shot Remington rifle and

Frank James (top) with hat in hand, about the time of his marriage in 1874. Jesse James (right) at age 28, taken about a year after his marriage to his cousin Zerelda in 1875. When it comes to hardware, Frank James states that he prefers Remington pistols (see the 1875 Remington revolver inset) because they are "the hardest and surest shooting pistol made."

– COURTESY ROBERT G. McCUBBIN COLLECTION –

JESSE W. JAMES.

Trained as guerrilla fighters in the border conflict between Kansas and Missouri, this loose group of ex-rebels formed a criminal confederation after the Civil War that seemed beyond the reach of the law. For almost two decades, the gang robs stagecoaches, trains and banks throughout the South. Only after they travel north, to what they believe will be "easy pickings," does the gang meet its downfall in a small town ironically called Northfield.

hits Bob Younger's horse, which is tied in front of the bank. Struck in the neck, the animal drops in its tracks.

Four horsemen ride back and forth, firing at any who dare to show their face. Instead of cowering, the locals come out with everything they have: Flintlocks, fowling pieces with mismatched ammunition, birdshot plunkers, frying pans and rocks. One pesky storekeeper even aims an empty pistol to draw fire and taunt the brigands. A Swede named Gustavson, who doesn't speak English, comes out of a cellar saloon and is shot in the top of his skull after failing to respond to one robber's command. (He dies several days later.)

Suffering from his face wounds, Miller remounts and pulls out his pistols. As he turns his horse to ride up Division Street, he is hit again, the bullet severing the outlaw's subclavian artery, and he falls to the ground in a heap. Cole rides over to Miller and dismounts. Quickly rolling his comrade over, Cole sees the blank stare of death stamped on Miller's bloody face. As he leans over Miller, a bullet rips into Cole's left hip. The elder Younger grabs Miller's two revolvers and remounts. Birdshot and buckshot whistle past his ears as Cole again rides to the bank door and pleads for the boys to leave. "I could not imagine what was keeping them so long," Cole later said.

Hearing the incessant firing from the street and the multiple pleadings of Cole, the robbers inside the bank become increasingly desperate. (See p. 60, "Inside the Bank.")

Seeing a chance to escape, teller Alonzo Bunker dashes out the back door and is chased by Charlie Pitts. Firing twice, Pitts hits Bunker in the shoulder, but the banker escapes. With their plan unravelling at every turn, the outlaws finally heed Cole's third call and prepare to leave.

Outside, local A.R. Manning bravely steps from behind the stairway at the corner of Scriver's and takes quick aim at outlaw Bill Chadwell (a.k.a. Stiles). Manning fires, and Chadwell topples from his horse, shot through the heart. (Manning is also the one who shot Cole in the hip.)

"For God's sake come out," Cole pleads from the doorway of the bank, more desperate than ever. "They are shooting us all to pieces."

Pitts, Bob Younger and Frank James finally emerge from the bank. (The last robber to leave climbs on the counter, turns and fatally shoots a stumbling, semi-coherent Joseph Heywood in the head. Bob immediately runs to the corner to confront Manning and several other townsmen. (Some sources claim Bob is merely heading for his horse, which has already been shot dead by Manning). While Bob plays hide-and-seek with Manning through the openings of Scriver's stairs, an upper-story shot from across the street rips into Bob's right arm, breaking the bone at the elbow. Undeterred, he deftly shifts his pistol to his left hand and continues firing.

As the others flee, Cole rides directly into the line of fire to pick up his little brother. A bullet severs one of Cole's bridle reins, forcing him to guide his mount with his knee and hand. As he turns his horse for Bob to climb aboard, Cole is hit in both the side and shoulder. His hat is also shot off. Another bullet rips away the back of his saddle. (One account reports Cole urges his brother to run, then picks him up a block away.)

The six wounded men give a meek rebel yell as they head south out of town. Although they survived the Battle of Northfield, their painful ride has just begun.

★

A rarely published photo of the Northfield battlefield, taken in 1876, the year of the attempted robbery. The view looks south on Division Street, straight into the scene of the fight. The Dampier House is on the left, with the third-story windows from which Henry Wheeler fires. On the far right is the staircase that A.R. Manning and other citizen shooters use to their advantage. Note the many wagons and lack of saddle horses.

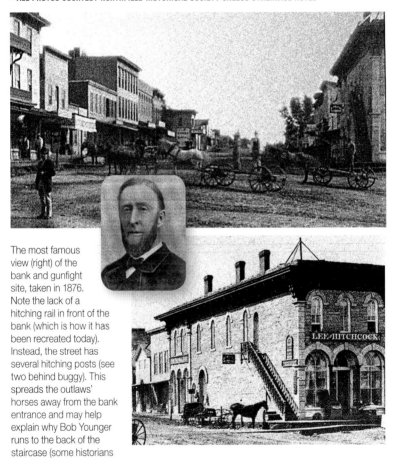

The most famous view (right) of the bank and gunfight site, taken in 1876. Note the lack of a hitching rail in front of the bank (which is how it has been recreated today). Instead, the street has several hitching posts (see two behind buggy). This spreads the outlaws' horses away from the bank entrance and may help explain why Bob Younger runs to the back of the staircase (some historians speculate he is trying to get to his horse). As Bob attempts to draw a bead on Manning, he is shot by Wheeler (see the shot angle in the top photo). Using his single-shot Remington rifle (below), Manning (inset) kills Bill Chadwell and Bob Younger's horse, and he wounds Cole Younger in the hip.

– REMINGTON RIFLE, BELOW, COURTESY EMF CO., INC. –

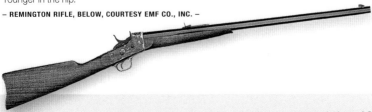

Theodore Roosevelt holding his favorite hunting rifle (the "Centennial Model" 1876 Winchester) during his tenure as a Dakota Territory rancher.

– COURTESY LIBRARY OF CONGRESS –

experiences in the Dakota Territory would forever shape his life and political career, and the adjacent national park encompasses the land he so loved. There are three units to the park: North (near Watford City), Elkhorn Ranch (Roosevelt's ranch), and South (adjacent to Medora). The south unit's scenic drive, many pullouts and trails provide visitors a beautiful overview of the park and opportunities to see wildlife, including bison.

330 Pacific Ave, Medora 58645
701-623-4830
MedoraND.com / NPS.gov

Upper Missouri tribes in North American history. Trails lead from the headquarters to culturally important and fragile village sites preserved in the park.

564 County Rd 37, Stanton, ND 58571
701-745-3300 • *NPS.gov*

Medora and Theodore Roosevelt National Park

Among the most beautiful—and entertaining—places in North Dakota are the inexorably connected restored historic village of Medora and Theodore Roosevelt National Park. Every summer the town of Medora comes alive as the community celebrates the legacy of Theodore Roosevelt at the *Medora Musical.* Frenchman Marquis de Mores founded the town in 1883 and named it for his wife. The Marquis's settlement also attracted another New Yorker, Teddy Roosevelt, who built a cattle ranch nearby in 1883. Roosevelt's

South Dakota

Badlands National Park

The wild, windswept Badlands National Park is 244,000 acres of buttes and ridgelines that have eroded over millions of years. Enjoy the Badlands Loop Road, with its pullouts, interpretive signs, endless vistas and wildlife. Stop at the Ben Reifel Visitor Center to learn the story of the Badlands and stay at the Cedar Pass Lodge. Want to visit the neighboring Pine Ridge Reservation? Stop at the White River Visitor Center, which is staffed by the Oglala Sioux Parks and Recreation Authority.

25214 Ben Reifel Pl, Interior, SD 57750
605-433-5361 • *NPS.gov*

Black Hills

Legendary and sacred, the Black Hills of western South Dakota remain as

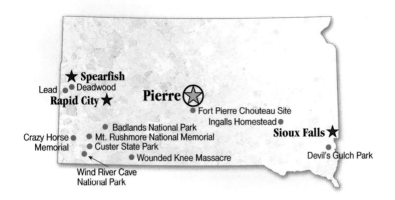

magnificent as they are mysterious, a premier Old West destination with thousands of years of history, innumerable trails to follow deep into its wild mountains and home to four of the most significant sites in the West: Custer State Park, Crazy Horse Memorial, Mt. Rushmore National Memorial and Wind Cave National Park. Whether you camp, stay at a historic lodge, guest ranch or inn, a visit to the Black Hills will inspire the Western traveler to come back many times to see the bison herd in Custer State Park, gaze upon the visages carved in granite at Mt. Rushmore and Crazy Horse, and walk deep in the sacred earth at Wind River Cave.

1851 Discovery Cir, Rapid City, SD 57701
605-355-3700 • *BlackHillsBadlands.com*

Deadwood and Lead

The epicenter of the Gold Rush of 1874-'76 that transformed the Black Hills, Deadwood was founded to supply the rush of miners everything they needed to survive: supplies, saloons and soiled doves. Visitors who walk the streets of Deadwood today should start at the visitors center in the restored railroad station for a map of the city, directions to local museums, daily events, historic sites and the Mt. Moriah Cemetery, where Wild Bill Hickok and

Calamity Jane are buried side by side. After touring Deadwood, drive up the mountain to tour the historic gold mining town of Lead.

501 Main St, Deadwood, SD 57732
800-344-8826
160 W Main St, Lead, SD 57754
605-584-1100
Deadwood.com / LeadMeThere.org

Devil's Gulch Park

On September 7, 1876, the James-Younger Gang was thwarted in their attempt to rob the First National Bank in Northfield, Minnesota. With multiple posses chasing them west out of Minnesota, the gang split up. Legend has it that soon after crossing into South Dakota, near Garretson, Jesse was separated from Frank, and while pursued, he avoided capture by leaping the 20-foot chasm of Devil's Gulch.

5th St & North Central Ave
Garretson, SD 57030
VisitGarretson.com

Fort Pierre Chouteau Site

In the 1830s, the American Fur Company had Frenchman Pierre Chouteau build a fort to serve the region, quickly becoming one of the most important trading posts on the Upper Missouri. After visiting the Fort Pierre Choteau Site, tour the

Whatever class of ticket these pioneers had, they faced a tough journey while traveling on this stagecoach from Deadwood, Dakota Territory, circa 1880.

Vérendrye Museum and the Vérendrye Site, where French explorer Pierre Gaultier De La Vérendrye placed a lead plate in 1743 claiming the Mississippi River drainage for France. After Fort Pierre, cross the Missouri River to Pierre and tour the State Capitol complex and the South Dakota Museum/Cultural Center.

About one mile north of Fort Pierre off SD Hwy 1806 on Fort Chouteau Rd
South Dakota Historical Society
605-773-3458 • *HistoricPierre.com*
HistorySD.gov

Ingalls Homestead

The Charles and Caroline Ingalls Homestead near DeSmet was started in 1880 after Laura Ingalls's family moved temporarily to the town in 1879. Readers of Wilder's books will recognize it from

her book *By the Shores of Silver Lake.* Laura married Almanzo Wilder in 1885. Today, visitors can tour a one-room schoolhouse, take a covered wagon ride, participate in hands-on crafts and pony-cart rides. Camping at the homestead can even be enjoyed in a covered wagon.

20812 Homestead Rd
De Smet, SD 57231
800-776-3594 • *IngallsHomestead.com*

Wounded Knee Massacre Memorial

The Wounded Knee Massacre Memorial Site on the Pine Ridge Reservation is a very solemn place. Visitors to the memorial should start at the Oglala Lakota College Historical

Center (open June-August, Monday-Saturday). Proceed to the Pine Ridge Area Chamber of Commerce in Kyle for information on visiting Wounded Knee (inquire about a guided tours). Afterwards, tour the Journey Museum & Learning Center in Rapid City, home to the Sioux Indian Museum, the SD Archeological Research Center and the Minnilusa Pioneer Museum to experience a broader understanding of culture and history in the region and state.

Wounded Knee, SD 57794
605-867-2228
NPS.gov / LakotaMail.com
OLC.edu / JourneyMuseum

The Ghost Dance religious ceremony that swept through the West with hope and promise in 1889 and 1890, ended in calamity and horror with the U.S. Army's massacre at Wounded Knee on the Pine Ridge Indian Reservation in December 1890.

– TRUE WEST ARCHIVES –

In 1873, Timothy O'Sullivan accompanied Lt. George H. Wheeler on his survey across the Four Corners of Arizona, Utah, Colorado and New Mexico. His talent as a photographer is equaled by his talent to recognize the significance of his subject matter, including the ancient Zuni Pueblo in New Mexico Territory.

– LIBRARY OF CONGRESS –

Great Books

American Carnage: Wounded Knee, 1890 *by Jerome A. Greene* (University of Oklahoma Press, 2015)

Black Elk: The Life of an American Visionary *by Joe Jackson* (Farrar, Straus and Giroux, 2016)

Deadwood *by Pete Dexter* (Random House, 1986)

Encounters at the Heart of the World: A History of the Mandan People *by Elizabeth A. Fenn* (Hill & Wang, 2014)

Homesteading the Plains: Toward a New History *by Richard Edwards, Jacob K. Friefeld and Rebecca S. Wingo* (University of Nebraska Press, 2017)

Hugh Glass: Grizzly Survivor *by James D. McLaird* (South Dakota Historical Society Press, 2016)

Hunting Trips of a Ranchman & The Wilderness Hunter *by Theodore Roosevelt* (Modern Library Classics, 1998)

James J. Hill: Empire Builder of the Northwest *by Michael P. Malone* (University of Oklahoma Press, 1996)

Solomon D. Butcher: Photographing the American Dream *by John E. Carter* (Bison Books, 2016)

The Female Frontier: A Comparative View of Women on the Prairie and the Plains *by Glenda Riley* (University Press of Kansas, 1988)

The Heart of Everything That Is: The Untold Story of Red Cloud, An American Legend *by Bob Drury and Tom Clavin* (Simon & Schuster, 2013)

The Lance and the Shield: The Life and Times of Sitting Bull *by Robert Utley* (Henry Holt & Co., 1993)

They Called Him Wild Bill: The Life and Adventures of James Butler Hickok *by Joseph G. Rosa* (University of Oklahoma Press, 1974)

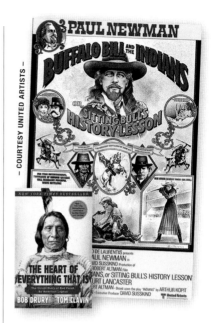

Classic Films & TV

7th Cavalry (*Columbia, 1956*)

Buffalo Bill and the Indians, or Sitting Bull's History Lesson (*United Artists, 1976*)

Crazy Horse (*TNT, 1996*)

Custer of the West (*Cinerama, 1967*)

Deadwood (HBO, 2004-2006)

Little Big Man (*National General Pictures, 1970*)

Little House on the Prairie (*NBC, 1974-1983*)

Man in the Wilderness (*Warner Bros., 1971*)

O Pioneers! (*CBS, 1992*)

The Emigrants (*Warner Bros., 1971*)

The Great Northfield Minnesota Raid (*Universal, 1972*)

The Homesman (*Roadside Attractions, 2014*)

The Revenant (*20th Century Fox, 2015*)

The Long Riders (*United Artists, 1980*)

Wild Bill (*United Artists, 1995*)

"Wild Bill" Hickok wears a butt-forward double holster rig in this photograph of him. This holster style allows for his fast draws in his various gunfights. When he slams his hands on the back of his pistols, they throw forward out of the holster, allowing for Wild Bill to whip the pistols around into firing position.

Wild Bill Cashes In

August 2, 1876

Wild Bill Hickok walks from his camp on the edge of Deadwood, Dakota Territory, to the Lewis, Nuttall and Mann's No. 10 Saloon. Entering around noon, he encounters about a half-dozen men. Three men are playing draw poker. Wild Bill recognizes Missouri River steamboat captain William R. Massie and Charlie Henry Rich, a card dealer Wild Bill knows from his days in Cheyenne, Wyoming Territory. Wild Bill joins their game.

Wild Bill sits in the only available seat, near the rear entrance of the saloon, facing the front door. He usually sits along the west wall, but Rich is occupying that seat. Wild Bill prefers that seat's view of the entire room, including good views of the front and back doors, and asks Rich for his "regular" seat, but the gambler refuses to move.

Wild Bill, uncomfortable with the fact that his back is exposed to the open bar and rear door, once again asks Rich to trade places. This time, the other players chide Wild Bill, telling him he has nothing to worry about this early in the day. Wild Bill takes the empty seat.

The four men have been playing draw poker for almost three hours when Jack McCall (also known as Bill Sutherland) walks through the front door, heads over to the bar, pauses, then moves down the length of the bar, stopping momentarily at the scales sitting on the end of the bar.

Wild Bill throws down his hand in disgust and says, "The old duffer, he broke me on that hand."

McCall steps forward, pulls a pistol from his clothing and points it at the back of Wild Bill's head, pulling the trigger at the same instant.

The bullet exits out Wild Bill's right cheek near the bottom of his nose. His head moves slightly forward, and he is still for a moment. Then he falls sideways off his stool onto the floor.

He dies instantly. ★

Jack McCall

Alias: Bill Sutherland

Age: About 25 years old when he kills Wild Bill

Home: Uncertain; either Jefferson Town, Kentucky, or New Orleans, Louisiana

Description: "His head which is covered by a thick crop of chestnut hair, is very narrow...a small sandy mustache covers a sensual mouth. The nose is what is commonly called 'snub'. Cross-eyes and a florid complexion." Also noted: "coarse double chin is partially hidden by a stiff goatee." At his trial, he is clad in a blue flannel shirt, brown overalls and heavy shoes.

DEADWOOD

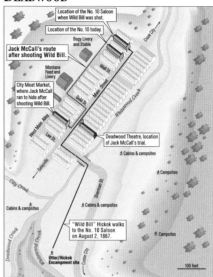

Location of the No. 10 Saloon when Wild Bill was shot.

Location of the No. 10 today.

Bogy Livery and Stable

Jack McCall's route after shooting Wild Bill.

Montana Feed and Livery

City Meat Market, where Jack McCall ran to hide after shooting Wild Bill.

Deadwood Theatre, location of Jack McCall's trial.

Cabins & campsites

Campsites

"Wild Bill" Hickok walks to the No. 10 Saloon on August 2, 1867.

Cabins & campsites

Cabins & campsites

Campsites

Utter/Hickok Encampment site

100 feet

THE NO. 10 SALOON

The original No. 10 Saloon apparently ceased to exist after the spring of 1877. An auction and consignment furniture store appears to have occupied the site sometime shortly after Billy Nuttall purchased and operated the Bella Union Variety Theatre next door.

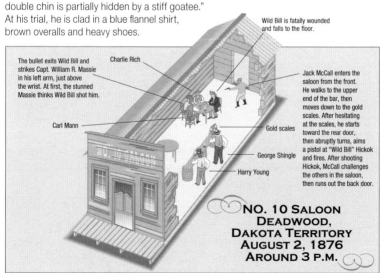

Wild Bill is fatally wounded and falls to the floor.

The bullet exits Wild Bill and strikes Capt. William R. Massie in his left arm, just above the wrist. At first, the stunned Massie thinks Wild Bill shot him.

Charlie Rich

Jack McCall enters the saloon from the front. He walks to the upper end of the bar, then moves down to the gold scales. After hesitating at the scales, he starts toward the rear door, then abruptly turns, aims a pistol at "Wild Bill" Hickok and fires. After shooting Hickok, McCall challenges the others in the saloon, then runs out the back door.

Carl Mann

Gold scales

George Shingle

Harry Young

NO. 10 SALOON
DEADWOOD,
DAKOTA TERRITORY
AUGUST 2, 1876
AROUND 3 P.M.

Dodge City was founded in June 1872, just three months before the arrival of the Santa Fe Railroad. Front Street's notorious establishments eagerly served buffalo hunters and cowboys whatever they desired. Today, visitors can walk the wild avenue's re-created boardwalks and storefronts at the Boot Hill Museum.

Southern Prairie and Plains

Arkansas, Kansas, Louisiana, Missouri, Nebraska

The Southern Prairie and Plains states should be considered the gateway states to the West. From the lesser-known trails to Texas and Oklahoma from Louisiana and Arkansas to the great epicenters of national trail history in St. Louis, Independence and St. Joseph, Missouri, the trails offer heritage travelers historic routes for transcontinental trips from Missouri on National Historic Trails as far away as Santa Fe, New Mexico, Sacramento, California, and Astoria, Oregon. In Kansas and Nebraska respectively, the vistas of the Great Plains inspire visitors to follow the famous Santa Fe and Oregon Trails westward, while inviting tourists to stop and explore the historic sites associated with the great cattle drives and military Indian War campaigns. Travel in the Southern Prairie and Plains region ties together the national story of the Trans-Appalachian West with the Trans-Mississippi West and how the competing empires of Spain, France, Great Britain and the United States vied to wrestle control of North America from the indigenous American Indian tribes.

Sod House in Custer County, Nebraska

The Visitor Center of the Fort Smith National Historic Site is located in the fort's former barracks, prison and Judge Issac Parker's federal courthouse and jail, which he presided over from 1875-'96.

Arkansas

Fort Smith Belle Grove Historic District

Belle Grove, one of the most significant historic districts in Arkansas, is a 22-block area of homes dating back 130 years adjacent to Fort Smith National Historic Site and the Arkansas River. Four homes are open for public tour: The Clayton House, McKibben-Bonneville House, Fort Smith Art Center and the Darby House.

Fort Smith CVB: 2 North B St
Fort Smith, AR 72901
479-783-8888 • FortSmithAR.gov

Fort Smith National Historic Site

In the annals of American Trans-Mississippi history, Fort Smith, founded in 1817, was an important gateway city to the West. While Missouri's St. Louis, Independence and St. Joseph receive more attention in the history books, Fort Smith's role in the development and settlement of Western territories, including Oklahoma, Texas and Kansas, must be considered. The National Park Service's Fort Smith National Historic Site is one of the largest, best-preserved interpretive centers of a historic 19th-century federal post west of the Mississippi. Tours should begin at the Visitor Center in the fort's former barracks/courthouse/ prison. Fort Smith may have been best known as the court of Judge Isaac Parker, the hanging judge. Visitors can tour the 37-acre grounds of Fort Smith on a 1.4-mile self-guided tour of all the key historic structures and sites, including the Gallows, Commissary and Trail of Tears National Historic Trail Overlook.

Fort Smith CVB: 2 North B St,
Fort Smith, AR 72901
479-783-8888 • NPS.gov

Historic Washington State Park

Founded on George Washington's birthday in 1824, Washington, Arkansas, is a National Register of Historic Places site, and one of the best preserved Southern villages west of the Mississippi River. Historic Washington State Park includes 30 preserved and restored architecturally important buildings constructed between 1824 and 1900. Numerous exhibits and collections can be enjoyed in the buildings open to the public, with re-enactors acting as hosts and guides. Start at the Visitor Center and inquire about programs, activities and tours of the historic town.

103 Franklin St, Washington, AR 71862
870-983-2625
HistoricWashingtonStatePark.com

Pea Ridge National Military Park

Known as the "battle that saved Missouri for the Union," Pea Ridge National Military Park preserves and interprets across 4,300 acres one of the most significant, and lesser-known major engagements of the Civil War in northwestern Arkansas. On a late winter day, March 27, 1862, 26,000 Union and Confederate soldiers clashed in one of the wars' largest Western battles. When the smoke cleared, the Federal forces had thwarted the Southern army from taking control of northern Arkansas and advancing into Missouri. Begin a tour at the Visitor Center's museum, where visitors can sign up for guided tours in the summer. One of the best ways to see the battle is to drive the park's interpretive loop, but the park also has walking and horse trails. Contact the park for a schedule of re-enactments and events.

15930 E Hwy 62, Garfield, AR 72732
479-451-8122 • *NPS.gov*

Prairie Grove Battlefield State Park

The Battle of Prairie Grove was significant in the history of the Western Theater of the Civil War. One of the most intact battlefields of the War Between the States, Prairie Grove Battlefield State Park preserves the site that left 2,700 dead or wounded in northwest Arkansas on December 7, 1862. Visitors may need more than one day to walk the battlefield trail, take the driving tour, visit historic Ozark Village and tour the park's museum and visitor center in Hindman Hall. A biennial event, the Battle of Prairie Grove Re-enactment will be held 5-17, 2018. Inquire with the park for more information.

506 E Douglas St,
Prairie Grove, AR 72753 • 479-846-2990
ArkansasStateParks.com

Kansas

Condon Bank Building

Rivaling the James-Younger Gang's failed bank robbery in Northfield, Minnesota, is the Dalton Gang's disastrous attempt to rob two banks, C.M. Condon and First National, simultaneously in Coffeyville, Kansas, on October 5, 1892. Convenient for visitors to Coffeyville, the area's Chamber of Commerce is located in the original site

of the C.M. Condon Bank, the 1871 Perkins Building, in the city's historic district. The chamber is open Monday to Friday and the bank vault, tellers' area and lobby can be seen as they were on that fateful day. From the Perkins Building, take a walking tour of the district to the Dalton Defenders Museum. The graves of Bob and Grat Dalton and Bill Powers can be visited in Coffeyville's Elmwood Cemetery.

807 Walnut, Coffeyville, KS 67337
620-251-5500 • *CoffeyvilleChamber.org*
DaltonDefendersMuseum.com

Constitution Hall

The history of Kansas is inexorably tied to both the development of America's expansion westward to the Southwest, Great Plains and the Northwest, and to the national political debate on the abolition of slavery and the Civil War. Historic Lecompton should be on everyone's tour of key heritage sites related to the Kansas-Missouri Border War. Constitution Hall was built in 1856 and is where the Kansas Territorial government first convened and wrote a pro-slavery constitution. After two years of conflict with Kansas anti-slavery factions, the seat of power was wrested from Lecompton's leaders and moved to Lawrence. Visit Constitution Hall, the Territorial Capital Museum or its website for information on a self-guided tour of the historic city.

319 Elmore St, Lecompton, KS 66050
785-887-6520 • *LecomptonKansas.com*

Dodge City

"The Queen of the Cow Towns," Dodge City's iconic status stands equally with that of Deadwood, Lincoln and Tombstone. A tour of Dodge City should begin at the Visitor Information Center for an orientation and guide to the city. Take the Historic Trolley Tour (Memorial Weekend to Labor Day), pick up a map of the Dodge City Trail of Fame and visit the internationally acclaimed Boot Hill Museum. Boot Hill is known for its outstanding exhibits on frontier Kansas history, firearms, gambling, buffalo hunters and the Wild West era of cattle drives. Visitors will enjoy walking amongst the historical interpreters and watching gunfight re-enactments on Front Street and the Variety Show in the Long Branch Saloon. While in Dodge City, don't miss a visit to the Gunfighters Wax Museum, and the Wild West Heritage Foundation's Buffalo and Longhorn Exhibit.

620-225-8186 • *VisitDodgeCity.org*

Fort Hays State Historic Site

First constructed in 1866, Fort Hays served the strategic needs of the U.S. Army in Western Kansas at three different sites until it was decommissioned in 1889. Commanders included Nelson Miles and Phil Sheridan, and was garrisoned by the 5th Infantry, 7th Cavalry and 10th Cavalry regiments, the latter a unit of Buffalo Soldiers. From 1867 until 1869, Maj. Gen. Sheridan and Lt. Col. George A. Custer were headquartered at Fort Hays in their war with the Southern Cheyenne and Kiowa people. Visitors will enjoy regularly scheduled re-enactment events, rangers in period dress, a museum and walking tours of the parade ground and four historic buildings.

1472 U.S. Hwy 183 Alt, Hays, KS 67601
785-272-8681 • *KSHS.org*

Fort Larned National Historic Site

The Army troops posted at Fort Larned were known as "the guardians of the Santa Fe Trail." Built in 1859, the outpost's buildings were constructed of native quarried sandstone, the reason Fort Larned National Historic Site remains one of the best-preserved Western outposts in the United States. Fort Larned is a living history center, with rangers and docents in period dress providing daily and monthly educational programs about life at a frontier Army post. Guided tours held May-September of the best way to learn the history of Fort Larned.

1767 Kansas 156, Larned, KS 67550
620-285-6911 • *NPS.gov*

Old Abilene Town

Abilene was founded in 1857, but it was the arrival of the Kansas Pacific Railway in 1867 that transformed Abilene into the legendary town at the end of the Chisholm Trail from Texas. Old Abilene Town is dedicated to promoting and preserving the colorful and popular heritage of the "wickedest and wildest" cow town of all the Kansas cow towns. Visitors to Old Abilene Town will enjoy re-enactors in period costume, gunfight re-enactments, special events and stagecoach and steam engine rides. Three other notable museums not to miss when visiting Abilene, Kansas: Dickinson County Heritage Center, the Dwight D. Eisenhower Presidential Library, Museum and Boyhood Home and the Historic Seelye Mansion.

100 SE 5th St, Abilene, KS 67410
785-479-0952 • *AbileneCityHall.com OldAbileneCowtown.com*

Medicine Lodge Treaty Site

The Medicine Lodge Treaty Site National Historic Landmark in Kansas is as important as Fort Laramie National Historic Site in Wyoming in understanding how the United States government negotiated with the Plains Indian tribes for land ownership and rights in the 19th-century settlement and conquest of the Indian Nations West. The historic importance of the three treaties is honored every two years by the Medicine Lodge Treaty Association at the Medicine Lodge Treaty Indian Summer Days.

Medicine Lodge Indian Peace Treaty Association
P. O. Box 194, 103 E Washington
Medicine Lodge, KS 67104
620-886-9815 • *PeaceTreaty.org*

A street scene in Abilene, Kansas, circa 1890s, with a medicine show drumming up business. It's interesting to note that this crowd is similar in size to the one Hickok faced when he confronted Coe.

– TRUE WEST ARCHIVES –

Louisiana

Chalmette Battlefield Site

On January 9, 1815, Gen. Andrew Jackson led U.S. forces over the British in a resounding victory to end the War of 1812 at Chalmette Battlefield Site (Battle of New Orleans) now Jean Lafitte National Historical Park and Preserve. Visitors to the national park can walk the field of battle and learn how Jackson's victory changed the course of history for the United States and the world. Tour the informative museum at the Battlefield's Visitor Center before enjoying the self-guided tour and visit to the Chalmette Monument, a 100-foot obelisk with 122 interior steps to the top. A unique way to visit the park is by the Creole Queen paddlewheeler from New Orleans' French Quarter; inquire with the park for information.

8606 W St Bernard Hwy
Chalmette, LA 70043
504-281-0510 • NPS.gov

Confederate Memorial Hall Museum

The influence of the Southern United States and the Confederacy on the

The National Historic Landmark Pontalba Buildings were built in the 1840s on Charles Street across from Jackson Square in the French Quarter of New Orleans, Louisiana, circa 1937.

– FRANCES BENJAMIN JOHNSTON, COURTESY LIBRARY OF CONGRESS –

settlement, politics and war in the American West is a critical part of the story of 19th-century America. Opened in 1891 in New Orleans's Warehouse District, the Confederate Memorial Hall Museum is dedicated to honoring Southern history.

929 Camp St, New Orleans, LA 70130
504-523-4522
ConfederateMuseum.com

The 1850 House

In New Orleans's Jackson Square, the 1850 House museum is dedicated to the family history of Baroness Micaela Almonester de Pontalba, whose father, Don Andres Almonester y Roxas, funded the construction of St. Louis Cathedral. The Upper and Lower Pontalba Buildings are considered the oldest apartment houses in the nation. The museum has

Spring Street Historical Museum
★ Shreveport   ★ Vicksburg

Fort St. Jean Baptiste Historic Site

Baton Rouge ✪

Confederate Memorial Hall Museum

The 1850 House
New Orleans ★

Chalmette Battlefield Site

re-created one of the residences to mirror middle class life in antebellum New Orleans.

523 St. Ann St
New Orleans, 70116
504-524-9118
The1850House.com

Fort St. Jean Baptiste Historic Site

The French were in Natchitoches in west-central Louisiana trading with local Indians as early as 1699. The trading post on the Red River was founded in 1714 and Natchitoches was the oldest city in the Louisiana Purchase. The Fort St. Jean Baptiste Historic Site reconstructs the French fort built in defense of the Spanish Empire. When in the area, don't miss a tour of historic Natchitoches, and the nearby Fort Jesup State Historic Site, built under the leadership Lt. Col. Zachary Taylor as a key American outpost between the Red and Sabine rivers in 1822.

155 Rue Jefferson
Natchitoches, LA 71457
318-357-3101 • *Natchitoches.net*
Crt.State.LA.us

Spring Street Historical Museum

The Shreve Town Company founded Shreveport to develop a town at the crossroads of the Texas Trail and the Red River in 1836. The development led to the opening of the river as a navigable waterway for steamships with the clearing of the Red River's infamous Great Raft logjam. The Spring Street Historical Museum exhibits provide an informative and educational window into the history of the Louisiana city which served as a gateway to the West.

525 Spring St, Shreveport, LA 71101
318-424-0964
SpringStreetMuseum.com

Visitors to Jean Lafitte National Historical Park and Preserve can walk the Chalmette Battlefield Site where Gen. Andrew Jackson defeated the British in the Battle of New Orleans in 1815.

– TRUE WEST ARCHIVES –

Missouri

Gateway Arch and Old Courthouse Building

St. Louis's Gateway Arch, an internationally recognized landmark of the "Gateway City," is the centerpiece of the city's historic district. Currently, the Museum of Westward Expansion, located under the Gateway Arch is closed for major renovations, and visitors wanting to visit the Arch should go to the Old Courthouse Ticket Center. The Old Courthouse is one of the most significant historical sites in Missouri, with several galleries dedicated to St. Louis's history, and the river city's role in Westward Expansion and Southern history.

11 N 4th St, St Louis, MO 63102
314-655-1700 • *GatewayArch.com*
NPS.gov

Wild Bill's Last Fight

October 5, 1871

The summer cattle season is all but over, and Marshal Wild Bill Hickok has kept the peace in Abilene, Kansas—not an easy job. The last marshal, legendary Thomas J. Smith, was killed in the line of duty.

Hickok is not popular with the Texans, having cleaned out the brothels the month before, on the order of the city council.

About 50 cowboys want to attend the city's Dickinson County Fair. When heavy rain sullies that venue, the boys wander from saloon to saloon on the main drag, bullying and intimidating patrons into buying them drinks. Some accounts suggest the cowboys pull this trick on Hickok, sweeping him off his feet and carrying him into the nearest saloon. Hickok humors the boys and buys them a round.

WILD BILL HICKOK

– ILLUSTRATIONS BY BOB BOZE BELL –

Rumors swirl that Texas gambler Phil Coe has sworn to get Hickok "before the frost." Many citizens make themselves scarce as the evening wears on, fearful that things may get out of hand.

At about nine p.m., Hickok hears a shot fired outside the Alamo Saloon. He earlier warned the cowboys against carrying firearms, so he confronts the

Wild Bill returns fire, mortally wounding gambler Phil Coe in front of the Alamo Saloon. News reports claim at least 50 cowboys were gathered on the street at the time of the shooting; the reports imply that several were injured by ricochet bullets.

group standing in front of the Alamo and encounters Phil Coe, with a pistol in his hand. Coe claims he fired at a stray dog, but as he says this, he pulls another pistol and fires twice, one ball going through Hickok's coat and the other thudding into the ground between his legs. Hickok reacts in a flash and "as quick as thought," according to the Chronicle, pulls his two Colt Navy revolvers. He fires them, hitting Coe twice in the stomach.

Others in the crowd are hurt. When another man brandishing a pistol emerges from the shadows, Hickok, not recognizing him in the glare of the kerosene lamps and his nerves on high alert, instinctively fires. He kills Michael Williams, a personal friend of his and a one-time city jailer.

Hickok carries Williams into the Alamo, and lays him down on a billiard table, then turns and disarms everyone he can find. The marshal warns them all to clear out of town. Within an hour, the place is deserted. ⭐

Wild Bill's remorse.

Abilene, Kansas, was a wicked and wild cowtown when Hickok resided there. The 1871 cattle season ended with drovers facing financial losses. Some pushed their herds on to Waterville, while others held their cattle in Abilene. They hoped for higher prices, but a shortage of freight cars kept the prices low, leaving the drovers with little choice but to sell short or winter them. Either way, many cow men were in a sour mood.

– TRUE WEST ARCHIVES –

Mark Twain Historic District
Jesse James Home
St. Joseph Historic District
Pattee House Museum
James Farm
Independence Historic District
Kansas City ★ Westport Landing
Jefferson City ⊛
★ St. Louis
Gateway Arch& Old Courthouse Building
★ Springfield

Jesse James Home/ Patee House Museum

Located on the grounds of the Patee House Museum stands the Jesse James Home, where the famous outlaw was shot and killed by Robert Ford on April 3, 1882. The Patee House was built as a hotel in 1858, was the headquarters for the Pony Express in 1860-'61 and was occupied by the Union Army during the Civil War. A National Historic Landmark, the Patee House has a superior collection of exhibitions dedicated to 19th-century Missouri life. The Jesse James House has an exhibit on Jesse James's life in St. Joseph and his grave.

1202 Penn St, St. Joseph, MO 64503
816-232-8206
PonyExpressJesseJames.com

Independence Historic District

The original trailhead of the Santa Fe Trail, historic Independence on the Missouri River remains one of the most important and influential frontier cities that shaped America's expansion West. Start your visit to Independence at the Visitor Experience Center and then take a self-guided walking tour of Independence Square. While in Independence be sure to see where Frank James was incarcerated at the 1859 Jail & Marshal's Home; visit the National Frontier Trails Museum; and schedule a covered wagon tour with Pioneer Trails Adventures.

112 W Lexington
Independence, MO 64050
816-325-7890 • *CI.Indpendence.MO.us*

James Farm

Until 1978, the James Farm was owned by descendants of the famed outlaw Jesse James. Today, the historic site in Kearney, Missouri, is a Clay County Museum dedicated to the James Family, the history of the region, the Border War and the Jesse and Frank James years as outlaws. The Visitors Center and Museum is in the restored 19th-century family home.

21216 Jesse James Farm Rd
Kearney, MO 64060
816-736-8500 • *JesseJames.org*

In 1877, Jesse and Frank James's family still lived and worked the land on their farm near Kearney in Clay County, Missouri. Today, the James Farm is a museum dedicated to the famous family's notorious—and tragic history.

– TRUE WEST ARCHIVES –

Born Samuel Langhorne Clemens in Florida, Missouri, November 30, 1835, the young future Mark Twain's family moved to Hannibal, Missouri, when he was four years old. Today, visitors to the Hannibal Historic District should start their tour of Twain country at The Mark Twain Interpretive Center.

Mark Twain Historic District

Walk the streets of historic Hannibal and a visitor can imagine a young Samuel Clemens growing up in the town and playing by the the Mississippi River. Start at the Mark Twain Boyhood Home and Museum, which includes eight historic properties, for a complete immersion into the real life of Twain. Tour the Mark Twain Interpretive Center and discover how the great American author transformed his own life and friends into the imaginary lives of his novel's fictional characters. Two tours not to miss: Mark Twain Cave and the Mark Twain Riverboat cruise on the Mississippi.

120 N Main St, Hannibal, MO 63401
573-221-9010
ExploreHannibal.com
MarkTwainMuseum.org

St. Joseph Historic District

Known best as the trailhead for the Pony Express, St. Joseph's historic district will inspire the imagination and

Rock Creek Station in Nebraska served as a Pony Express and Overland Stage stop but is probably best remembered for a shootout involving Wild Bill Hickok.

remind visitors of the importance of Missouri's western frontier towns to American history. Begin tours of historic St. Joseph at the Pony Express Museum, followed by a visit to the extraordinary St. Joseph Museum, with its extensive displays on the culture and history of the region, including American Indian and Civil War exhibitions. Also, don't miss the Patee House Museum, Jesse James Home, Robidoux Row Museum and Pony Express Monument.

St. Joseph CVB, 109 South 4th St
St. Joseph, MO 64501
800-785-0360 • *StJoMo.com*

Westport Landing

While St. Louis, Independence and St. Joseph receive more attention from historians—and have more historic sites associated with the Western trails—Westport Landing was actually the site that wagon trains and wagon train bosses preferred for many years to prepare and provision for the transcontinental journey to Oregon or Santa Fe. Visit the Harris-Kearney House Museum managed by the Westport Historical Society in the Kansas City suburb of Westport and learn about life in the 19th-century frontier town and its role in the development of the West.

4050 Pennsylvania Ave, Suite M100
Kansas City, MO 64111 • 816-531-4370
WestportHistorical.com

Nebraska

Buffalo Bill State Historical Park

Buffalo Bill State Historical Park preserves Scout's Rest Ranch, the home of the great Western showman William F. "Buffalo Bill." Cody first began ranching in the area in 1877 and began building a major farm and ranch operation in North Platte in 1878. A major enterprise, the Nebraska ranch was home to Cody and his family for many years. He owned the property until 1911. The park includes the Cody House and barn. The ranch is also noted as the place Cody debuted his Wild West show, known as the Old Glory Blowout, in 1882.

2921 Scouts Rest Ranch Rd
North Platte, NE 69101
308-535-8035 • *VisitNorthPlatte.com*
OutdoorNebraska.gov

Chimney Rock
National Historic Site

A landmark for travelers in the North Platte River Valley for chimney rock in the Sand Hills of western Nebraska, is today protected as Chimney Rock National Historic Site. The unique geological site is just east of Scotts Bluff, another significant landmark in the area. Explorers, fur trappers and emigrants used the landmarks to guide them as they traveled the Oregon Trail. Chimney Rock is managed by the Nebraska Historical Society and includes a Visitor Center Museum.

Chimney Rock Trail, Bayard, NE 69334
308-586-2581 • *NebraskaHistory.org*

Chimney Rock National Historic Site near Bayard, Nebraska, protects the famous landmark that was used to guide travelers going east and west on the Oregon Trail.

– COURTESY NATIONAL ARCHIVES AND RECORDS ADMINISTRATION, NO. 294354 –

Fort Kearny
State Historical Park

Fort Kearny State Historical Park preserves and promotes the history of the U.S. Army's role in protecting the Overland Trails along the Platte River in central Nebraska. Founded in 1848, Fort Kearny served the region until 1871. In 1928, the Fort Kearny Historical Society bought 40 acres for a park and rebuilt key structures: the stockade, powder magazine, carpenter-blacksmith shop and the parade grounds. The park has an interpretive center and hosts living history events throughout the year.

1020 V Rd, Kearney, NE 68845
308-865-5305
OutdoorNebraska.gov

Fort Robinson
State Park

Fort Robinson State Park is one of the most historically significant—and largest—state parks in Nebraska. Near Crawford, with dozens of historical buildings and museums on site, Fort Robinson encompasses 22,000 acres, with numerous houses and camping spots for rent. Fort Robinson was founded in 1874 and served the Army until 1947. Fort Robinson was involved in critical events of the Great Sioux War, including as the site where Crazy Horse surrendered and was later

After the Civil War, the Homestead Act enticed homesteaders to follow the old trail out onto the prairie and stake out a piece of the American dream.

– SOLOMON D. BUTCHER, CA. 1887, LIBRARY OF CONGRESS –

killed, the Dull Knife breakout of the Northern Cheyenne and the Fort Robinson Massacre.

Soldier Creek Rd, Crawford, NE 69339
308-665-2900 • OutdoorNebraska.gov

Homestead National Monument of America

The Homestead National Monument of America in Beatrice, Nebraska, honors the history of homesteading and the men, women and families who staked so much on 160-acre homesteads with the hope of building an independent life and future. Tours should begin at the Heritage Center, which has an excellent museum, followed up by an outdoor tour of the park, including the Education Center, Palmer-Epard Cabin and Freeman School.

8523 NE-4, Beatrice, NE 68310
402-223-3514 • NPS.gov

Rock Creek Station State Historical Park

Rock Creek Station State Historical Park is the site of the stagecoach station where James Butler "Wild Bill" Hickok had his shootout with Dave McCanles. Working as a stock boy, Hickok fueded with the local McCanles ending with Wild Bill's enemy dead, and beginning a Western legend's career as a gunfighter.

57426 710th Rd, Fairbury, NE 68352
402-729-5777 • OutdoorNebraska.gov

Scotts Bluff National Monument

Scotts Bluff National Monument is dedicated to interpreting the culture, heritage and history of Scotts Bluff and the North Platte River Valley. During the early 19th-century, European and American fur trappers plied the paths along the North Platte to and from the West, marking a key trail that would guide the way West for successive generations of emigrants. Tours of the park should start indoors at the Visitor Center, but the strength of the monument is in its numerous trails, including the Oregon Trail Pathway and the North and South Overlook.

190276 Old Oregon Trail
Gering, NE 69341
308-436-9700 • NPS.gov

Great Books

Andrew Jackson and the Miracle of New Orleans: The Battle That Shaped America's Destiny *by Brian Kilmeade and Don Yeager* (Sentinel, 2017)

Cowboy's Lament: A Life on the Open Range *by Frank Maynard, ed. by Jim Hoy* (Texas Tech University Press, 2010)

Dodge City: Wyatt Earp, Bat Masterson, and the Wickedest Town in the American West *by Tom Clavin* (St. Martin's Press, 2017)

Dodge City and the Birth of the Wild West *by Robert Dykstra and JoAnn Manfra* (University of Kansas Press, 2017)

Empire Express: Building the First Transcontinental Railroad *by David Howard Bain* (Viking, 1999)

Isaac C. Parker: Federal Justice on the Frontier *by Michael J. Brodhead* (University of Oklahoma Press, 2003)

Pioneer Women: Voices from the Kansas Frontier *by Joanna L. Stratton* (Simon & Schuster, 1981)

Pony Express *by Fred Reinfeld* (Bison Books, 1973)

Shot All to Hell: Jesse James, the Northfield Raid, and the Wild West's Greatest Escape *by Mark Lee Gardner* (William Morrow, 2013)

The Buffalo Soldiers: A Narrative of the Black Cavalry in the West, revised edition *by William H. Leckie with Shirley A. Leckie* (University of Oklahoma Press, 2007)

The Santa Fe Trail: Its History, Legend, and Lore *by David Dary* (Knopf, 2000)

The Year of Decision: 1846 by Bernard DeVoto with an introduction *by Stephen E. Ambrose* (St. Martin's Griffin, 2000)

Wagons West: The Epic Story of America's Overland Trails *by Frank McLynn* (Grove Press, 2002)

– COURTESY WARNER BROS. –

Classic Films & TV

Abilene Town (*United Artists, 1946*)

Dodge City (*Warner Bros., 1939*)

Gunfight at the O.K. Corral (*Paramount, 1957*)

How the West was Won (*MGM, 1962*)

Kansas Raiders (*Universal, 1950*)

My Antonia (*USA Network, 1995*)

The Adventures of Huckleberry Finn (*MGM, 1939*)

The Assassination of Jesse James by the Coward Robert Ford (*Warner Bros., 2007*)

The Big Trail (*Fox, 1931*)

The Buccaneer (*Paramount, 1958*)

The Comancheros (*20th Century Fox, 1961*)

The Great Northfield Minnesota Raid (*Universal, 1972*)

The Gunfight at Dodge City (*United Artists, 1959*)

The Homesman (*Roadside Attractions, 2014*)

The Jayhawkers (*Paramount, 1959*)

The Long Riders (*United Artists, 1980*)

The Outlaw Josie Wales (*Warner Bros., 1976*)

The President's Lady (*20th Century Fox, 1953*)

True Grit (*Paramount, 1969*)

True Grit (*Paramount, 2010*)

Wyatt Earp (*Warner Bros., 1994*)